Soul Provider

Tim Elmore

First Printing, January 1992
Second Printing, February 1992

Published by
HERE'S LIFE PUBLISHERS, INC.
P. O. Box 1576
San Bernardino, CA 92402

Cover design by David Marty Design
Interior design by Genesis Publications

Library of Congress Cataloging-in-Publication Data
Elmore, Tim.
Soul provider : becoming a confident spiritual leader / Tim Elmore.
p. cm.
ISBN 0-89840-344-8
1. Men—Religious life. 2. Christian leadership. I. Title.
BV4843.E58 1992
248.8'42—dc20 91-36764
CIP

For More Information, Write:

L.I.F.E.—P.O. Box A399, Sydney South 2000, Australia
Campus Crusade for Christ of Canada—Box 300, Vancouver, B.C., V6C 2X3, Canada
Campus Crusade for Christ—Pearl Assurance House, 4 Temple Row, Birmingham, B2 5HG, England
Lay Institute for Evangelism—P.O. Box 8786, Auckland 3, New Zealand
Campus Crusade for Christ—P.O. Box 240, Raffles City Post Office, Singapore 9117
Great Commission Movement of Nigeria—P.O. Box 500, Jos, Plateau State Nigeria, West Africa
Campus Crusade for Christ International—100 Sunport Lane, Orlando, FL 32809, U.S.A.

What Men Are Telling Men About SOUL PROVIDER . . .

"I encourage you to read, ponder, and follow the principles and exercises within this consequential book. *SOUL PROVIDER* combines the author's passion for godliness with workable tools for the young laborer or the experienced veteran in the body of Christ."

John C. Maxwell
Senior Pastor
Skyline Wesleyan Church

"At long last, a book that tells men why they should—and how they can—become real spiritual leaders at home! The message is biblical, practical and commonsense, wrapped in loving concern which manifests itself in specific action steps that are easy to apply. You will benefit from reading it."

Zig Ziglar
Author and Speaker

"A long-awaited help in the area of spiritual leadership, *SOUL PROVIDER* is a down-to-earth, practical approach. One of Tim Elmore's strengths is his insight on immediate application. These truths can restore health again to our homes, churches and workplaces."

Josh McDowell
Author and Speaker

"More and more men are asking experienced leaders, 'How can I learn to lead—both right and well?' Tim Elmore is helping to answer this question."

Jack Hayford
Senior Pastor
The Church on the Way

"I have greatly enjoyed the good effects of the Skyline Wesleyan ministry of which *SOUL PROVIDER* is a part . . . an important subject presented practically by a practicing author."

Fred Smith
Author and Speaker

"I highly recommend this book! It is must reading for every man who is grappling with being a spiritual leader not only on the homefront but also in the workplace."

Ron Jenson
Higher Ground Associates

This book is dedicated to my wife and girlfriend, Pam, whose unconditional love has provided an excellent laboratory for learning how to become a spiritual leader.

A Special Thank You

Rarely is a book project a "one man show." This piece is no exception. I wish to express my gratitude for the contributions made by the following friends/co-workers . . .

To Steve Kelsey for his wisdom and insight into both the assembly and content of this project.

To John Maxwell for teaching me leadership, then opening the doors of opportunity for me to become one.

To Joyce Hendren for her tireless efforts on the computer, and always with a smile on her face.

To Kent Askew for building a hunger in me to both study and become a spiritual leader, as a man.

To Tim Warkentin for being a patient "sounding board" and for gently sharing his thoughts along the way.

And to the whole Skyline congregation for providing such a beautiful family setting to learn these truths.

Contents

PAST HURT
REBELLION!
IGNORANCE
PRIDE
Apathy

Foreword

A quick trip at a fast clip through any bookstore easily discloses voluminous self-help books. It's definitely a seller's market for authors profiting from the "wanna-be's." *Soul Provider* is not a "wanna-be" book. It is instead a guide for the willing person with a hungry heart and sincere desire to pay the price to become a spiritual leader.

The work that Tim Elmore has completed in this volume declares his own spiritual leadership birthright and his mastery in successfully transferring these principles to others. One word comes to my mind that causes Tim to stand alone as an exceptional author on this topic: passion. Tim savors the fullness of his relationship with Jesus Christ. It is that love affair with Jesus that compels others to follow Tim as he follows Jesus. To be a good leader one must be a good follower.

The body of Christ is in need of spiritual leadership—especially confident male leadership. Why is there such a deficiency? If it is the price, corporately the church pays dearly for the lack of it. If the process, is not the journey worth the reward? If pride, have we overlooked the benefits of brokenness Jesus mirrored? Whatever it is, surely the absence of noticeable spiritual leadership has contributed to the church's impotency and lack of influence among the secular.

Traveling across the country speaking on leadership, I am often asked many questions about the subject. How do I identify a leader? How can leadership be developed in others? Why do some avoid leadership? But the most heartfelt question comes from wives: "Why isn't my husband more of a spiritual leader at home?" Our homes, families, and churches are in despairing need of godly male authority. I have observed and resolved that effective male leadership is not often inherent but can be learned.

If spiritual leadership can be learned, why the lack? In the Great Commission passage, Matthew 28:18–20, we read that Jesus was given "all authority." Those who are in Christ have access to that same authority. We believers live far below our privilege in Christ and have not appropriated the power the Holy Spirit has gifted us with. Fear of changes, fear of failure, or fear of pain paralyzes our hearts and faith. I encourage you to read, ponder, and follow the principles and exercises within this consequential book.

My longing is that *Soul Provider* would capture your heart and your head. Desire and knowledge are wonderful companions because they pull together and make a strong union. This book combines the author's passion for godliness with workable tools for the young laborer or the experienced veteran in the body of Christ. Reader, whatever the expanse of your leadership in God's kingdom, *you are a leader*. Someone is watching you, following you, modeling you. I encourage you to take the journey and become a significant spiritual leader and influencer—*for Jesus' sake*.

DR. JOHN C. MAXWELL
Senior Pastor
Skyline Wesleyan Church

To the Reader

Let me be honest with you about who my target is.

In a broad sense, this material was written for anyone who desires to be a spiritual leader, whether male or female, young or old, single or married. It has been used by each of these types of people with success: The reader discovered the material to be helpful and relevant for his or her life.

However, it is my hope that men grasp the truths in this book most of all. Cultural and sociological trends have made it common for men to feel inadequate, intimidated, or ignorant of what it means to be a spiritual leader. Clearly, there is a vacuum of those who model it for us. Men have become passive in relationships, which has led to broken families, inhumane business practices, and unhealthy churches.

I envision this material being used in at least four contexts:

1. Personal study. You read and interact with the content on your own, and implement the ideas suggested.
2. Accountability partnership. You and a partner(s) form a couplet or triad and work through the lessons.
3. Small group discussion. A cell group meets regularly to discuss the content in a casual group setting.
4. Sunday school class. A class (of singles or couples) studies the material together, as a series.

Whatever you do, may I encourage you to do one thing: Decide now that you are going to implement the truths presented, and become a practicing spiritual leader to those in your sphere of influence.

TIM ELMORE

CARE
LEADERSHIP

1

Why Do I Always Get the Tough Job?

Men often confess they know how to excel in nearly every other area of their lives except this one.

It was a scene you may identify with.

There he was, seated in my office with a look of confusion on his face. He was engaged to be married, yet was struggling over several areas in his relationship with his fiancée. They had dated long enough to get beyond the "goose bumps" of infatuation. They believed they were experiencing real love—but it was work. And to heighten the pressure, he knew that many of the issues that needed to be resolved in the relationship required change and growth on *his* part.

Finally I drew my conclusion, like a gun before a duel: "It's quite simple," I said. "You need to become a spiritual leader." I smiled at him as though I had just discovered the key to unlocking all of his problems, as though I had given him news he'd been awaiting for years. And I was right; he *did* need to become a spiritual leader with his partner. But his response was less than enthusiastic.

"I've been told that at least a dozen times by Christians who know me. But not once has anyone ever stopped to share just how I can become one!"

It was humbling to hear those words. He was right, at least in my case. I had dished out that advice hundreds of times without ever offering the hows or whys.

This time, however, I knew I had to do something about my advice. That "something" has become the essence of these pages. It is my objective to define what is meant by the term "spiritual leader"; to build a biblical foundation for our convictions; and to give practical insights on how one becomes a spiritual leader in relation to his wife, his family, his church, and his workplace.

I will attempt to address questions such as:

- What does God expect from men? From husbands?
- How do I develop the qualities of a spiritual leader?
- Why is it often difficult for men to lead in relationships?
- How can I be an authentic spiritual leader and still be me?
- What does a spiritual leader do?

In the chapters that follow, we will journey through an exciting adventure of growth—full of risks and rewards. The format is designed to be very straightforward—I am assuming you are a "bottom line" person and want to get to it without a lot of wasted words. The format is designed to be fun as well. I trust it will be just that for you. Each chapter has opportunities to write out your thoughts and conclusions and to apply what you've read. At the end of each chapter is a "Developing a Lifestyle" section that presents ideas for exercises on becoming a spiritual leader within your relationships. I encourage you to commit yourself to this application. Spiritual leadership should be much more than a cognitive experience; it's not so much what you *know* as what you *do*.

The applications in this book are enhanced if you are involved in a committed relationship, whether it's with a spouse or fiancée. If you are single, I encourage you to choose someone (of either sex) to be a sounding board and a source of accountability as you work through this material. You'll have a place to write the name of this person at the conclusion of this chapter.

Obviously, you are beginning your journey through this material because you sensed the need for it, or because *someone* in your life suggested that it would be helpful. Maybe it was both. Why not pause for a moment right now and prayerfully request that God would continue to build a teachable spirit in you, and that He would make you the person He wants you to be?

The Tough Job

As a pastor, I have been surprised that more material has not been written on this crucial subject. No doubt it's a tough one to write about, much less live out. Ironically, most churches today do not offer any kind of support ministries that equip men for the task. We have largely avoided the subject. My guess is that the dearth of resources is partly because we are unsure of the job description of a "spiritual leader." It's a tough role, made tougher because it's difficult to specify exactly what a guy does to become one. But this lack of resources is not the only reason for this book.

Let me share with you why I believe this is the time to address the subject of becoming spiritual leaders. The following are four simple observations I've made.

1. Spiritual leader is a tough role to play.

No doubt about it, being a spiritual leader in today's world is difficult. Not only do we live in a highly immoral and unholy society, but we've experienced a leadership gap produced by the decade of the 1960s. During that period America seemed to shun leadership and the "establishment" in favor of demonstrations and discussion groups. The result is that the men of today have seen an absence of strong leadership. We don't know how to do it, since we've had so few models. We've seen political leaders fall morally; religious leaders and televangelists have crumbled by the dozens; business leaders have exhibited a pitiful set of ethics; and more than half of our homes in America are broken ones.

2. Spiritual leadership is being requested by women.

It has been interesting to observe the cycle of requests made by females regarding the males of their generation. One divorced woman in our church commented, "Make our men strong again! First they were too domineering; then they were too weak. Where are the men who know how to both lead and love?" The well-known columnist "Dear Abby" received a letter with this disclosure and request: "I'm single, I'm forty years old, I'd like to meet a man about the same age who has no bad habits." Abby simply replied, "So would I."

It is true. Men tend to be one extreme or the other: dominant or passive. Denise, a good friend of mine, told me, "We women really do hunger for men to be spiritual leaders. But because so few of them know how, we tend to take control of the relationship. Eventually, though, we do it out of resentment." Another woman, Kim, elaborated on this when she spoke of her fiancé. "Now that I am in a relationship with a spiritual leader, I can't see it working any other way. It's like night and day. His gentle but firm leadership has sparked an intimacy and a security that I've never experienced before. He is investing in me as a person—and that is the greatest way to communicate love that I know of."

3. Spiritual leadership has become a "hot button" for men.

As I travel, I often pose the question to men, "What's the greatest need in your personal life right now?" The majority of the time both married and single men will reply, "I need to be a spiritual leader." I often meet men who've become successful business professionals who confess they know how to excel in nearly every other area of their lives except this one. Furthermore, because they tend to get more "strokes" of encouragement from the areas in which they do well, they spend more time working at the office than leading in the home.

I have observed some very clear symptoms in the men I work with at our church in San Diego. All the symptoms are cries for someone to show them how to become the role model they were meant to be. First, I see a spiritual hunger in men. They are blatantly requesting that someone demonstrate leadership and godly relationships. As I write this, my desk is covered with letters from men either asking for material or thanking me for sending some to them. It's a bit scary because I don't see myself as an expert at all—it's just that the hunger is so real. Second, I see a feeling of inadequacy in men. They feel guilty for not living as they should, but helpless to make any changes on their own. Third, I see fear and intimidation in many of them. They're afraid that as they do find out what spiritual leadership means, it will require risks they are unable or unwilling to take.

4. Spiritual leadership is desperately needed in the church.

I don't think I need to elaborate much on this truth. Fewer men than women are involved in America's Protestant/ Evangelical churches, and of the men who are active, even fewer practice spiritual leadership. Someone once said that if the Holy Spirit were removed from our church ministries,

95 percent of the activities would continue unchanged. We must begin again to build men (and women) who live above the tyranny of the flesh, who understand more than programs and publicity, and who walk as spiritual models for those who look on.

The good news is, each of these four observations can be resolved. I firmly believe God wishes to build the men of this generation into spiritual leaders—so that churches will be changed and in turn become change agents, businesses will be transformed, and homes will be restored to the intended pattern.

Before we move on to the "meat" of the book, let me conclude with an encouraging letter I received. It was written by a woman whose husband had just attended a seminar containing the material you're about to read. I hope it whets your appetite . . .

> Dear Pastor Tim,
>
> My husband attended your Spiritual Leadership seminar last fall.
>
> I meant to write this sooner (do a preschooler and an infant count as excuses?) as I wanted to tell you how *much* the seminar helped him and our marriage. He was literally changed. (Still is!) He took the material to heart and God has blessed us incredibly through his leadership. We have an entirely new relationship.
>
> We were married as non-Christians at age 20. I accepted the Lord in June 1987 and he on the eve of our ninth wedding anniversary in November 1988. Until this seminar, the leadership role was not quite established and/or was unbalanced, but now—*wow*!
>
> Thank you for passing on this life-changing material to him. He has already shared it with another married friend. I hope he continues to do so.
>
> Thank you again.

Application

At the onset of this study, you are challenged to identify one person in your life who . . .

- knows you well
- is mature and objective
- you can talk to openly
- lives near you

It has been said, "Success is having credibility with those who are closest to you." Choose someone with whom you would most want to have credibility. It may be your wife, fiancée or girlfriend, or it may simply be a friend to whom you've chosen to be accountable.

Write this person's name in the space below:

____

In the following chapters, this person will be referred to as your "partner."

I'M THE SPIRITUAL LEADER AROUND MY HOUSE, AND I'M GOING TO PROVE IT!
THAT'S RIGHT--YOU SHOW 'EM WHO'S BOSS!

2

What a Spiritual Leader Is, and Is Not

Scripture lays a solid foundation for husbands to be spiritual leaders in their homes and in the church.

A friend and I were discussing a newspaper article last week that I have chuckled at more than once.

A young mother was running errands around town one morning, with her three preschool children corralled in the back seat of her car. It was a hectic day, so to keep the kids quiet she pulled into a Wendy's restaurant and purchased three kid's meals, complete with hamburger, fries, drink, and a toy. Upon receiving the food, one of her preschoolers whined, "Mommy, they didn't give me any hamburger in my bag!" She probed, and sure enough, no hamburger. This was frustrating because of her busy agenda, so she quickly turned her car around, sped into the parking lot, grabbed the Wendy's bag and entered the restaurant. She addressed the clerk behind the counter abruptly: "I just bought this Wendy's kid's meal, and there is no hamburger in it. Please put a hamburger in the bag." The clerk was so startled by the woman's demand that she just stood there. "I said," the mother repeated with clenched teeth, "I just bought this kid's meal and there's no hamburger in it. Put one in it *now*."

At this point, the clerk had caught on and raced back to the grill to obtain a hamburger. Upon giving it to her the young mother placed it in the Wendy's bag and promptly exited . . . the McDonald's restaurant!

What a woman! I laughed as I responded to my friend, "It's amazing what can be accomplished when you've got a purpose!" It really is true. Possessing a clear purpose accelerates achievement and growth. This chapter is, in effect, a "purpose" chapter. In it, I will examine the biblical foundation for spiritual leadership, offer a definition for it, and describe both what a spiritual leader is and what one is not. My hope is that in all this, you will align your life with the purposes of God as they relate to spiritual leadership.

Let's begin by going straight to the Bible.

Building a Biblical Foundation

Scripture lays a solid foundation for husbands to be spiritual leaders in their homes, and for men to offer spiritual leadership in the church. That is not to say that men are more spiritual than women. Often it is quite the contrary, and far easier to get women involved in positions in the church. Additionally, women are frequently needed to fill the void of spiritual leadership in homes and churches across our country. By the term "spiritual leader" we are simply referring to:

> "One who assumes responsibility for the health of the relationship or group."

We will discuss more about what this means later in this chapter. I believe after researching Scripture you will be convinced of the biblical basis for this definition, and how important it is for you to be one.

My objective in giving you these Scriptures is not to build an unrealistic image of the male as a controller. Instead it is to illustrate that God does not want you *passive* in relationships, as men often become, but initiating love and care toward others. This was your intended role from the beginning.

TRUTH IN A NUTSHELL: Genesis 2:7,18–25

- God formed man from the earth, and woman from the man.
- God's original purpose was for the woman to be a helpmate, a companion, and a complement to what was lacking in the man.
- It is safe to say that God thought man couldn't live well without the woman, and the woman without the man.

THINK IT OVER/WRITE IT DOWN . . .

How would a proper understanding of this Scripture change the way men and women respond to and view each other today?

TRUTH IN A NUTSHELL: 1 Timothy 2:11–14

- God, through the apostle Paul, tells us what happened in the Garden of Eden.

- The term *authority* (NASB) indicates a strength or right endued upon one by God. It denotes a position of responsibility more than superiority—and was given to man.
- Adam was given this position because he was created first, and because God chose to give it to him.

THINK IT OVER/WRITE IT DOWN . . .

How is this Scripture abused today by men? What is a balanced response to the truth of this text?

It is important to note that just as it is clear God wants man to assume this position of responsibility, God could have easily chosen to give it to the woman. Men are not more spiritual than women, as I have stated. God simply had created a world that required leadership at various levels (the earth itself, nations, churches, families, etc.) and thus sovereignly placed man in that position.

TRUTH IN A NUTSHELL: 1 Timothy 5:8

- This passage indicates the role of man in his own household to be that of a provider and caretaker.
- The word "provide" or "develop" means the male is to facilitate security and growth in his household.

THINK IT OVER/WRITE IT DOWN . . .

List a variety of ways a male could provide for or develop his partner and family. Be creative.

TRUTH IN A NUTSHELL: Ephesians 5:22–25

- Wives are to be subject to their husbands; husbands are to love their wives as Christ did the church; hence, mutual submission.
- Husbands are the Christ-figures in the relationship, carrying out the care, ministry and sacrifice that Jesus does.
- If husbands will love their wives in this manner, wives will generally have few problems submitting to this kind of love.
- God designed husbands to be the head or leader of the household (i.e., assuming responsibility for its health).

THINK IT OVER/WRITE IT DOWN . . .

If husbands are to love their wives just as Christ loved the church, what should they be doing? How did Christ love the church?

How much authority do you have in the lives of people closest to you? How have you earned it?

Do people find it difficult to submit to your leadership? Why or why not?

This passage, coupled with 1 Corinthians 11:3, defines a "chain of care" that God has given us:

- God
- Christ
- Church
- Husband
- Wife
- Children

It is important to note that these levels do not imply a chain of superiority. Christ is obviously equal with God, since He was and is God incarnate (Philippians 2:5–11). However, Jesus understood the chain of care or responsibility as He walked this earth and willingly submitted to God the Father as the One who was positioned over Him (John 6:38).

I recently provided marriage counseling to a young couple whose struggles revolved primarily around a misunderstanding. Neither understood their roles within the relationship. There was confusion concerning their sexual identity. He was attempting to assert a dominant, controlling façade; she was attempting to maintain her individuality and independence in response. She thought he was not being very Christlike. He thought she was completely ignorant of her biblical role as a wife. Finally he looked at me and asked, "Who's the head of the house?"

I'm sure he was hoping for me to spit out some Scriptures that would endorse his chauvinistic, dominating lifestyle. Instead I gently reminded him, "That's really not the kind of question a believer should even have to ask." The question believers should be asking is not "Who's the master?" but rather "Who's the servant?" When a man comes into an authentic understanding of his role as a spiritual leader, he doesn't become more bossy or controlling. He serves. In turn, this generally spawns a similar response from the Christian wife. Most wives, no matter how strong their own personality or leadership ability, will *welcome* a husband living out authentic spiritual leadership.

TRUTH IN A NUTSHELL: 1 Peter 3:7–9

- The apostle Peter speaks to husbands as the ones who are responsible for the health of the marriage relationship.
- Peter also defines the wife's role as one of submission. However, as much as we dislike talking about submission, that role is really the easier of the two. The toughest role is the husband's role: to love as Christ loves—which ultimately drove Him to the cross. I have a sneaking suspicion that if we, as men, would love our wives this way, they would have fewer problems submitting to our leadership.

THINK IT OVER/WRITE IT DOWN . . .

What does it mean for husbands to "be considerate as you live with your wives" (verse 7)?

As we take responsibility for these relationships, what are the directions Peter gives us in verses 7–9?

What Is a Spiritual Leader, Anyway?

Now that we have surveyed the heart of God (or the spirit of the law) behind masculine leadership, we must define what is meant by it. To what is God calling you as a spiritual leader? Before we define what a spiritual leader is and does, it would be wise for us to define what he is *not*. We must begin by destroying the stereotypes and distorted images we often possess about our role as men. Let's take a look at some of these common misconceptions. Jesus said that knowing the truth would make us free. I trust that the truth about these stereotypes and myths will do just that. After each one, reflect on it and answer the following two questions:

- How does knowing this truth free you?
- Will you need to change any behavior patterns in light of this truth? Which ones?

What a Spiritual Leader Is Not

1. **He is not a preacher.**
   You do not have to be an eloquent communicator who continually has nuggets of wisdom spilling out in your conversations. Nor does it mean you are to lecture the people in your family or sphere of influence.

2. **He is not a boss (dictator).**
   You are not to "lord" it over the people in your life, just because you are the spiritual leader. Jesus taught servant-leadership. God didn't call you, as a man, to be bossy, narrow or stubborn. You are not a dictator but a developer.

3. **He is not the Holy Spirit.**
   Don't confuse your role: You are to share God's love and the Holy Spirit is to convict. Not vice versa. You need not go around being a source of guilt for your partner by being "holier than thou."

4. **He is not a talker.**
   Being a spiritual leader does not mean monopolizing conversations, nor does it mean always having something pious to say on every topic that arises. You are as much a listener as a contributor in conversation.

5. **He is not an idealist.**
   Too often, men who attempt spiritual leadership in relationships become "hyper-spiritual." They become impractical and idealistic, forgetting that being a godly leader should make them more practical than ever.

Because there are relatively few men who reflect true biblical leadership, it is easy to slip into one of these stereotypes. Be sure to resolve these common misconceptions as you spot them in your attitudes.

What a Spiritual Leader Is

Now let's attempt to distill what a spiritual leader is. The following paragraphs comprise a brief list of qualities that mark a spiritual leader. Study and memorize these six words beginning with the letter "I" and make this your "I Can Do It" list.

1. Initiative

My wife appreciates this one. She loves it when she doesn't feel that she's the one always taking responsibility for progress in our home and marriage. Recently we began to discuss what we were going to do on our next "date night" (a regular time we take to enjoy each other alone). She said, "You decide what we're going to do." So I planned for us to be picked up in a chauffeur-driven Cadillac, for her to find a rose and her favorite beverage in the back seat, and for us to dine by the ocean at a beautiful restaurant. I poured it on. At the conclusion of our date, she remarked that her favorite part of the whole evening was not anything we did, but rather that I had simply cared enough to initiate it all. Evaluate yourself based on this summary of the quality of initiative:

- I give direction in my relationship with my partner.
- I take responsibility for the health of the relationship.
- I initiate spiritual dialog with vulnerability and humility.

Give an illustration of how you have done or will do this.

2. Intimacy

Another facet of spiritual leadership is the capacity to experience intimacy in relationships. In his book, *Honest to God*, Bill Hybels uses Mike Singletary (Chicago Bears all-pro linebacker) to illustrate godly manhood. He notes that Mike is strong enough to be revered by any opposing player, but sensitive enough to shed a tear as he displays affection for his wife and children.[1] This requires a heart that is both contrite (needing God and needing others) and courageous (willing to step out and be vulnerable about it). Evaluate yourself on the quality of intimacy:

- I experience intimacy with God through personal worship and study time.
- I experience intimacy with my partner through open and honest conversation.

Give an illustration of how you have done or will do this.

3. Influence

This is an often-abused quality. A generation of chauvinists drew the wrath of women who protested strong male influence. However, when another generation withdrew from attempting to assert any influence with women, even some feminists decided they wanted it after all.

For instance, Deborah Laake wrote, “Ten years ago we were complaining that men all feel this need to perform their macho role and think they've got to be strong and they can't cry. And now we've released them from that. We wanted to destroy sex roles, so we destroyed them, and now we're complaining."[2]

Evaluate yourself on the quality of influence:

- I exercise biblical influence within my relationships.
- I develop, encourage, and facilitate growth in my partner.
- I am a "giver," a generous contributor in relationships.

Give an illustration of how you have done or will do this.

4. Integrity

This is a hot button today. Not even some of our visible Christian leaders have been able to model it. Integrity means "oneness"—we are the same person no matter who is watching. The concept comes from a Latin root meaning "without wax." In ancient Roman culture, statues were fired in hot ovens that often would crack them. Wax was then used to fill those unattractive cracks. Every now and then, however, a statue would make it through the oven without any flaws—hence, no wax or any outside material was needed to cover a crack. It was just one substance. And at the bottom of those statues the sculptors would inscribe "without wax" (sinceros) or "integrity." In our lives this means authenticity, transparency, and absolute honesty. Evaluate yourself on the quality of integrity:

- I lead a life of integrity, honesty that is above reproach.
- I am not ashamed of my private life, of what I am when no one is looking.

Give an illustration of how you have done or will do this.

5. Identity

God requires that we develop a secure and healthy self-concept based on who He says we are in Scripture. Most of us falter in drawing our identity from Him because of lies we have believed while growing up. Zig Ziglar tells the story of a young boy named Victor who came to the U.S. with his Soviet parents years ago. He soon started school and was immediately isolated as dull and mentally slow. Both teachers and classmates openly remarked about his stupidity until Victor finally dropped out of high school in humiliation. He tried to make ends meet during the next several years. As fate would have it, Victor took an aptitude test at about age 30. To his surprise he discovered that his I.Q. was 161. He was a genius! His life changed almost overnight, and he has since become president of civic clubs, written books, married, and patented inventions. He began to live the life of a genius.[3] Now, did Victor become intelligent overnight? No. What changed his life was the way he saw himself. And the same thing should be happening to us spiritually as we begin to live by the identity God has given us in the New Testament. Evaluate yourself on the quality of identity:

- I am secure in who I am in Christ.
- I have a healthy, biblical self-image that prevents a defensive attitude.
- I have developed a mature statement of purpose for my life.

Give an illustration of how you have done or will do this.

6. Inner Character

This final quality deals with our moral and spiritual strength. How much do we exemplify Jesus? Do we display biblical convictions? I love the true story of two young men who were fighting together in World War II during 1944. They had grown up together, played together, worked together, and graduated together. They even ended up in the same platoon in Europe during the war. It was in the midst of a fierce battle that one of these two became upset. Their troop had returned behind the lines without his long-time friend. He told his commanding officer that he must go back into the front lines and find his friend. He just had to. He couldn't go on without attempting a rescue. The C.O. told him there was no use trying it, and if he did it would mean risking his life. But this wasn't enough to stop him. An hour later he returned with the lifeless body of his friend cradled in his arms. The C.O. scowled in anger, "You see, I told you it was useless to go out there." The young soldier looked up at him and responded, "That's where you're wrong, sir." There was a pause. "You see, I got to him just in time to hear him say, 'I knew you'd come.' It was worth everything to make it to him."

This kind of courage and character doesn't come easy. But it can come, and can be seen in any relationship in which you are involved and have invested yourself. Evaluate yourself on the quality of inner character:

- I exhibit the fruit of the Spirit in my life, which includes self-discipline.
- I am a Spirit-filled, Spirit-led believer.
- I maintain control by submission to God's and human authority.

Give an illustration of how you have done or will do this.

Where Do You Go from Here?

Now that you're aware of the qualities you need to develop, I am concerned that you not get discouraged. Although none of us are perfect, these ingredients are possible to possess. Otherwise God would not request them of us. And by His grace we will grow into them. For now, understand that knowing them is simply step one. I suggest you implement the exercises at the end of each chapter to begin practicing the qualities of spiritual leadership. Some will be easier than others.

In the following chapters, we will explore how you can become the spiritual leader you were intended to be. Fasten your seatbelts. This is going to be an adventure.

Developing a Lifestyle

- In the previous chapter you chose a partner, a person to be accountable to during this series. Pray with him every day this week, even if you have to do it over the phone.
- Spot your weakest quality from this lesson and list three action steps you can take to improve it.

  1. ______________________________

  2. ______________________________

  3. ______________________________

- In your own words, share with your partner a good definition of a spiritual leader.
- Memorize 1 Timothy 5:8:

  > If anyone does not provide for his relatives, and especially for his immediate family, he has denied the faith and is worse than an unbeliever.

3

The Functions of a Spiritual Leader

Spiritual leadership is more an issue of "heart" than of "art."

During World War II, the Battle of the Bulge called for every available man to be put into the line to stop the German drive. For the emergency, a unit consisting mainly of clerks and office workers was hastily converted to infantry and assigned to a section of road that was expected to be under fire within a matter of hours. They were issued shovels and told to dig foxholes. One man, whose life of operating a typewriter had left him unprepared for digging in stone-hard ground, asked a lieutenant, "Sir, wouldn't it be easier if we attacked and made them dig the foxholes?"

What a great question! Why not approach life in a completely different way? Why not initiate? Why not get on the offensive instead of waiting for someone else to take the first step forward?

The office clerk's question needs to be posed to men today in the context of the war for their families, their churches, their marriage relationships and their personal lifestyles. One woman commented recently, "It seems that twenty years ago, women were clamoring for their men to become soft and gentle, to back away from their take-charge posture and mellow out! Today, however, we're clamoring for them to lead again, to be strong and stand up for what needs to happen in the home." I think she's right. Men in general have become passive in giving meaning to relationships with family, the church, and even with each other. Men have backed down and allowed someone else (sometimes *anyone* else) to lead in relationships.

Examine, for instance, the churches during the early days of our country. During the eighteenth century, they were led primarily by men. Women were involved, of course, and necessary in the life of the church. But it was the norm for men to initiate and lead. By contrast, less than 250 years since then, it's often difficult today to get men to lead, to teach, and to shepherd in the local church. Whether it's because they feel unqualified or ignorant, too busy or unchallenged, men find it easy to grow passive—and limit their activities to discussing sports and weather in the fellowship hall.

According to surveys conducted by Lyle Schaller and by the research department at *Christianity Today*, men typically compose only about 35 to 40 percent of an adult congregation. In churches with attendance of one hundred or fewer, 81 percent have women's ministries and only 59 percent have men's.[1] The complexion of the average American church actually caters to the feminine gender, knowingly or unknowingly. Frequently the vocabulary, programming, and goals fail to challenge men or model Christ's call to radical discipleship, courage, boldness, strength, and sacrifice.

In addition, since many women are more articulate about their faith, men often hesitate to talk about spiritual matters, particularly around women. However, this does not mean men are less spiritual. It simply means our culture makes it easier for women to express religious interest than for men. Men have not been given a lot of help in fulfilling the role they're supposed to fulfill. "Men's jobs and families consume them," says journalist Mike Marcey. "They want to know how to be better fathers, better managers. But they have little time and energy to figure out how."

Being a spiritual leader in the home is frustrating for many men because they often are not equipped to function in that role. They feel insecure at home—tremendously inadequate sometimes. So what do many men do? Spend more time where they're succeeding (their jobs) and less time where they are not. And that just exacerbates the problem.[2]

Spiritual leadership means initiating in relationships. It involves taking the first step, even when it's a difficult or uncomfortable one. A friend of mine once took exception to these statements by saying, "Why should I take an uncomfortable step if my spouse is naturally better in that particular area? If her strength lies in that context, it seems silly for me to demand to lead there."

I agree. But being a spiritual leader (male or female) doesn't mean you claim to be better or stronger in every endeavor. Rather, it means you initiate the steps to ensure health in each context. If my wife is better at balancing the checkbook (which she is), I need not demand that I do that task. But I assume responsibility to ensure steps have been taken so our checks don't bounce! Leadership doesn't mean I do everything. It does mean I see to it that everything gets done. It's initiative.

This role and responsibility was never illustrated more vividly than by little Tony, who was just four years old at the time. He was walking with his daddy one evening when he stumbled and fell. Looking up at his father he asked, "Why don't you watch where I'm going?" Good question, Tony.

This leadership role is often a very quiet one. Initiative is frequently subtle. It's tending to the little things and being sensitive to the people closest to you. But, that's usually what is noticed. One woman from Naples, Florida wrote to "Dear Abby" and commented:

> Dear Abby,
>
> I love my husband. Let me tell you why:
>
> I love him for not making any noise when he gets up at 6:30 every morning and knows I like to sleep a little later.
>
> I love him for never asking me why I don't balance the checkbook.
>
> I love him for walking the dog and feeding the cat, even though they're both mine.
>
> I love him for not making me pay him off when I lose a bet, even though he always pays when he loses.
>
> I love him for not noticing when the beds aren't made.
>
> I love him for noticing when my hair is done a new way.
>
> I love him for being extra nice to my mom and dad.
>
> I love him for watching a 1956 romantic movie with me even though the Celtics are on the other channel.
>
> I love him for not getting mad when there's not a clean shirt in the drawer.
>
> I want him to know it's the little things that count.[3]

The Functions To Be Performed

Now that we have defined what a spiritual leader is and is not (Chapter 2), let's move on to discover the tasks of a spiritual leader and some practical steps to becoming the leaders we were meant to be. The following information is designed to present a variety of ideas to encourage you in living out the functions of spiritual leadership.

According to J. Oswald Sanders, the functions or tasks of a spiritual leader can fall under the following umbrellas:

- To serve
- To confront

- To guide
- To initiate
- To undertake responsibility[4]

THINK IT OVER/WRITE IT DOWN . . .

Which of these tasks is easiest for you in a relationship? Why?

Which of these is the most difficult for you? Why?

Is it easiest for you to "initiate" at work, at church or at home? Why?

Remember, the more difficult tasks are usually awkward because we are waiting for someone else to do them for us. Becoming a "giver" is essential. We don't initiate and give either because we're not letting *God* give to *us* in those areas, or because we are refusing to follow his pattern of giving. "For God so loved the world that He gave . . . "

Chuck Swindoll tells the story of a young orphan who was wandering the streets of England shortly after World War II came to a close.

> Early one chilly morning an American soldier was making his way back to the barracks in London. As he turned the corner in his jeep, he spotted the little lad with his nose pressed to the window of a pastry shop. Inside the cook was kneading dough for a fresh batch of donuts. The hungry boy stared in silence, watching every move. The soldier pulled his jeep to the curb, stopped, got out, and walked quietly over to where the little fellow was standing. Through the steamed-up window he could see the mouth-watering morsels as they were being pulled from the oven, piping hot. The boy salivated and released a slight groan as he watched the cook place them onto the glass-enclosed counter ever so carefully.
>
> The soldier's heart went out to the nameless orphan as he stood beside him.
>
> "Son . . . would you like some of those?"
>
> The boy was startled.
>
> "Oh, yeah . . . I would!"
>
> The American stepped inside and bought a dozen, put them in a bag, and walked back to where the lad was standing in the foggy cold of the London morning. He smiled, held out the bag, and said simply:
>
> "Here you are."
>
> As he turned to walk away, he felt a tug on his coat. He looked back and heard the child ask quietly:
>
> "Mister . . . are you God?"[5]

We are never more like God than when we give.

What Does Scripture Say?

Take a look at 1 Peter 5:1–4:

> To the elders among you, I appeal as a fellow elder, a witness of Christ's sufferings and one who also will share in the glory to be revealed: Be shepherds of God's

> flock that is under your care, serving as overseers—not because you must, but because you are willing, as God wants you to be; not greedy for money, but eager to serve; not lording it over those entrusted to you, but being examples to the flock. And when the Chief Shepherd appears, you will receive the crown of glory that will never fade away.

Peter is addressing the spiritual leaders of the church, but the principles are the same in personal relationships. Note that the tasks of a spiritual leader can be distilled further into four memorable words. We must *model, minister, mentor,* and *manage.*

1. Model

We are called to be a living model for those around us. The text specifically commands leaders to be "examples to the flock" (verse 3). The simple truth is that people do what they see, not necessarily what they hear "preached" at them. Our lives must align with our lip, or we give a confused message at best.

Years ago, there was a horrible train wreck along the Elizabeth River in North Carolina. Several passengers drowned as the train derailed off a broken piece of track overlooking the river. The flagman was accused of waving a white flag instead of a red warning flag that would have kept the train from this catastrophe. However, the flagman claimed with absolute certainty that it was not a white flag, but a red one—he was doing precisely what his job called him to do. Finally, someone suggested that the man produce the flag to resolve the debate forever. When the flag was examined, the reason for the confusion became clear. It was indeed a red flag, but had faded over time until it was a very pale color—sending no clear message at all. Often, I wonder if our lives aren't like that flag. We are waving our message in the faces of all who will watch and listen—but it's a faded message due to the weathering our lives have endured. And the world around us is confused at what we are really saying about the power of God to change lives. Do our lives look any different from theirs?

Yankee Hall-of-Famer Joe Dimaggio was once asked, "Why do you always play so hard?" Dimaggio replied, "It's just become a part of who I am." But when he was questioned again about why this was, he shared the real motive behind his effort: "Because I know there's always at least one person out there who's never seen Joe Dimaggio play before." I like that. In my own life, I have noticed a similar quantum leap toward excellence since I've become permanently conscious of my being watched. It's really made a difference.

2. Minister

Second, we are called to minister, to "be shepherds of God's flock," to serve those under our charge. It appears to be a paradox at first, but we lead by serving and we serve by leading.

My friend and employer, John Maxwell, was teaching the art of serving and ministering to his leadership board at Skyline Church in San Diego. He asked the men where they have the most difficulty serving: in their job, the church, or their home. The vote was unanimous: the hardest place to serve was in the home. Consequently, Pastor Maxwell gave them all an assignment. Beginning that week, each was to begin volunteering to do tasks, servanthood tasks, around the house—without any announcement that it was an assignment from the pastor. The men chuckled as they envisioned what might happen. And sure enough, during the next week Pastor Maxwell received several phone calls from wives who assumed something was up. They would generally begin by recounting some wonderful service their husband had rendered, then follow with the question, "What have you done to my husband?"

The truth was, he had done nothing more than remind those men that leadership begins with servanthood in the home.

3. Mentor

A third task is to mentor those under you. This involves the voluntary investment of your life in other people. It means developing them based on the proper motives of bettering them for God's purpose in their life, not yours (verse 2).

A classic illustration comes from two brothers at McGill University in Montreal, Canada. Thomas S. Steward injured one of his eyes with a knife. A specialist in eye surgery decided that it should be removed immediately to save the other eye. When the operation was over and Tom had recovered from the anesthetic, it was discovered that the surgeon had blundered by removing the healthy eye, thus making the man totally blind. It was a nightmare for both Tom and his family. However, despite the tragedy, he decided to continue pursuing law at McGill. He was able to do this only because of a decision his brother William made in his behalf. William decided to become a sort of mentor to his brother Tom. He read to him, coaxed him through all of his examinations, and literally accompanied him through the various phases of college life. The incredible part of this true story is this: blind Tom graduated at the top of his class, while his brother/mentor William finished second. But then, that sort of result is the reward of any mentor.

4. Manage

The final area of spiritual leadership is the call to manage. The text urges us to serve as overseers. This implies being a visionary, at least enough to see the big picture regarding those lives within our care/influence, and to facilitate their growth in light of that picture. This function requires not only the development of our organizational skills but the inward discipline of keeping alive the vision of who our children or spouse or friends are called to be. We must envision the end product if we expect it to become reality.

No one was a greater visionary than Walt Disney. Unfortunately, he died before the grand opening of Disney World, one of the many dreams he had labored to bring into being. Since Walt could not make the ceremonial speech, Mrs. Disney was called to the platform to speak. As she was introduced, the emcee remarked, "Mrs. Disney, I just wish Walt could have seen this!" She stepped to the microphone and with great resolve replied, "He did." And she sat down.

A Case Study: Boaz

Take a few moments and read the Old Testament book of Ruth. It is a beautiful love story between Ruth and a mature, healthy, quality spiritual leader. His name was Boaz. Note how Boaz conducts himself in the development of this relationship. After careful reading, you will see a narrative on the qualities we've just examined.

Cite an example(s) of how Boaz was a **model**:

Cite an example(s) of how he was a **minister**:

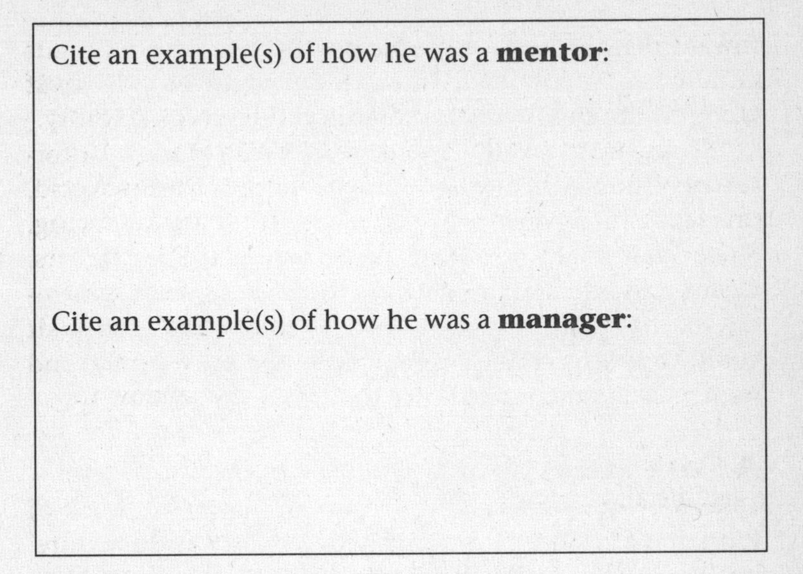
Cite an example(s) of how he was a **mentor**:

Cite an example(s) of how he was a **manager**:

The Heart of the Matter

It is important to underscore the fact that spiritual leadership is more an issue of "heart" than of "art." These functions will be futile if they are simply cosmetic, form, and technique. They must flow out of our being, not just our doing.

To ensure this, in his book *Spiritual Leadership*, J. Oswald Sanders gives us three intrinsic qualities to develop. All of our modeling, ministering, mentoring and managing must include these. Relationship partners will follow and respond to leadership that is . . .

- **Authoritative** (direction that is clear, decisive and confident)
- **Spiritual** (priorities that are godly, disciplined, Spirit-filled and Christlike)
- **Sacrificial** (giving that is centered on others, with surrendered rights)[6]

How did Boaz display these qualities?

Authoritative:

Spiritual:

Sacrificial:

Speaking the Truth In Love

Whether we are talking about relationships we have within our churches, our places of employment, our neighborhoods or our homes, we *must* prioritize and become proactive in building lines of communication with people. Author and pastor Bill Hybels writes:

> All of us long for deep, authentic relationships marked by integrity and open communication. But how often do we experience them? Occasionally? Once in a lifetime? Never?
>
> During the last decade and a half, I've heard many tales of relationships marred by hidden hostilities and unspoken hurts. While several factors contribute to this, I believe the biggest problem is that too often we

> violate the basic requirement of authentic relationships: honesty.
>
> Learning how to tell others the truth is the basis of genuine relationships.[7]

As a spiritual leader, you will be called upon at some point to be a truth teller when it is extremely difficult. Today's buzz word for such an occasion is *confrontation.* Let me give you a list of steps I've used when I have been called upon to confront a difference, hardship, attitude, or sin in someone:

1. Pray through your anger.
2. You initiate the contact.
3. Begin with affirmation.
4. Tell him *you* have a problem or struggle.
5. As you bring up the issue, explain that you don't understand why this is . . .
6. Establish forgiveness and repentance.
7. Compromise on opinions, not on convictions/principles.
8. Pray and affirm your love at the end.

As you can see, spiritual leadership separates the proverbial men from the boys. It challenges us to break completely out of our comfort zones and our human tendencies to be passive, pushy, or "plastic" around the home. And I believe both families and churches are crying out for this authentic leadership—imitators and fakes need not apply.

I heard recently that a new custom began in the nation of Burma just after World War II. For the first time, men allowed women to walk in front of them in public along the community roads. Was this an emerging gesture of courtesy or modern chivalry? Were the males finally developing into sophisticated gentlemen? Hardly. The truth was, there were land mines all around that had not yet been detonated! These men were not dummies!

While I have to chuckle at stories like this, I must also mention that at times our outward expressions of love and servanthood seem to be as artificial and self-centered.

Elements You Must Bring to the Relationship

Maybe an acrostic for the word "LEADERSHIP" will help summarize the elements you must bring to the relationship:

L – *Listening.* How could you display this?

E – *Encouragement.* How could you give this?

A – *Attitude.* How could you initiate a positive one?

D – *Demonstration.* How could you exemplify godliness?

E – *Equipping.* How could you develop your partner?

R – *Responsibility.* How could you take this on?

S – *Servanthood.* How could you model this?

H – *Humility.* How could you exhibit reliance on God?

I – *Inspiration.* How could you bring this to your partner?

P – *Priorities.* How could you initiate proper ones?

Try memorizing this acrostic; say it aloud once a day for an entire week. Hopefully, you'll find yourself seeing the whole picture in a much more definitive way.

Some Practical Steps for You

A good place to begin your leadership journey is in your home. As you concentrate on the four objectives in 1 Peter 5:1–4, begin to apply the following practical how-to steps.

MODEL

- Train yourself to continually ask the question, "What would Jesus do?"
- Be conscious of your example when with your partner.
- Open up and be transparent in conversation.
- Pray together.

Any others?

MINISTER

- Find out your partner's personal needs and attempt to meet the ones you can.
- Look for tangible ways to serve her when you're together, without calling attention to yourself.
- Forgive all wrongs and affirm her.
- Be sensitive and begin to anticipate her needs.

Any others?

MENTOR

- Initiate loving confrontation when there are barriers or offenses in the relationship.
- Discover your partner's gifts and help her find an outlet for them.
- Pray for her spiritual growth.
- Give constructive criticism.
- Read the same Scripture daily and find time to discuss what you both found.

Any others?

MANAGE

- With your partner's input, make decisions on what you will do on date nights.
- Assume responsibility to divide functions to be performed within the relationship.
- Be a peacemaker.
- Initiate maintaining a clear conscience in the relationship.

Any others?

Developing a Lifestyle

- Memorize 1 Peter 5:1–4.
- Of the four functions listed in 1 Peter 5—model, minister, mentor, manage—choose the one that is your weakest area, and concentrate on the practical steps listed on the previous pages.
- Plan an evening of fellowship with your partner. Go out to dinner this week, just the two of you, and serve her by your affirming words and actions—and by picking up the tab.

4

Barriers to Becoming a Spiritual Leader

Our weaknesses must be addressed before we will be free to become spiritual leaders.

I couldn't quite put my finger on why I didn't feel right about Bob and Susan. They both had attended my young adult class at church and had dated for over two years. But now that they were making plans for marriage, I became distinctly aware that something didn't fit. Call it intuition. Call it discernment. I just wish I could have explained it, because I knew this poor couple wanted to be married, or have some valid reasons presented to them if they shouldn't.

As I probed in our conversation together, it became obvious that Bob did not have a healthy home life growing up. His parents had been in and out of two marriages each. He grew up with an anxious mother and an absentee father. He remembered toughing things out alone during his school years.

All this was instrumental in who Bob had become. I noted his inability to be vulnerable, both with Susan and with me. He struggled with communication and avoided any hints of confrontation. Needless to say, these weaknesses had to be addressed before Bob would be free to become a spiritual leader.

Fortunately, Bob took some action, and God was able to bring healing and wholeness to his character over time. Both Susan and our church have benefited from Bob's wholeness and spiritual leadership in recent months. Unfortunately, this story is not as common as it should be. Steve and Janeice were in a similar predicament and Steve needed to face some issues himself. Instead, he chose to live in denial, and insisted that he and Janeice marry—right away. She realized within the first month of marriage that he had been wearing a mask of spirituality and maturity. By the end of year two, they were in the divorce process. I was tempted to say, "I told you so," but refrained. What Steve really needed was for someone to walk him through what I call a "truth journey." He had some barriers to overcome. The dysfunction of his past was hindering him from healthy relationships and spiritual leadership.

It's my guess that you might identify with some of Steve's barriers. These common barriers we face are frequently the source of our feeling . . .

- Indifferent
- Ignorant
- Intimidated
- Inadequate

about our role in the home or church. Before we study the ingredients that go into the making of a spiritual leader, it will be helpful to examine some of these common barriers that prevent us from being healthy leaders.

THINK IT OVER/WRITE IT DOWN . . .

Using your present understanding of spiritual leadership and considering your personal relationship with God, write down what you feel is the largest barrier to your becoming a spiritual leader.

Our greatest relationship role model in life has most likely been our parents or the home in which we were raised. God brought us into this world as helpless infants in the care of our parents who were to love, nurture and develop us. He didn't bring us into this world as complete, adjusted adults. He intended for the family to be the place where we began to understand *His* love in a safe and comfortable environment.

Mounting evidence and personal testimonies have revealed that what God intended as a model of His loving care has too often turned out to be a place of hurt, anger, fear and resentment. Even if your upbringing was relatively free from problems, your parents are only human and sometime during your childhood may have planted some wrong seeds that have resulted in unhealthy behavior patterns.

If we are to be effective spiritual leaders in our own relationships, we need to understand how God relates to us as Father and as our ultimate spiritual leader. In his article "The Father Heart of God," John Dawson discusses the critical facets of parenthood and how they may foster "misconceptions concerning God and His love for us."[1] As we examine some of these, I challenge you to take an honest look at your life growing up and see if your relationship with God has been hindered in any way due to a failure or lack of tender loving care from one or both of your parents.

Facets of a Father

1. Parental Authority

Abuse of authority is rampant today in all levels of society. Governmental and religious leaders, as well as leaders in the home, have abused the power and authority given them by God. I can still remember a family that lived down the street from me years ago. They bought a dog who absolutely loved people and loved life. His name was Rex. Rex was everybody's friend. But over the years, noticeable changes took place in his personality. Rex was living in a home where love was absent and authority was abused, and he just happened to be at the bottom of the totem pole. He was yelled at, smacked, and punished several times a day. I literally watched Rex change from an affectionate puppy to one who cowered in fear at the sight of any adult. The way he greeted people spoke volumes of the way authority was displayed in that home.

How do you approach God? Chances are, you will respond to God the Father the same way you responded to your parents.

THINK IT OVER/WRITE IT DOWN . . .

Read Hosea 11:1–4.

> When Israel was a child, I loved him, and out of Egypt I called my son. But the more I called Israel, the further they went from me. They sacrificed to the Baals and they burned incense to images. It was I who taught Ephraim to walk, taking them by the arms; but they did not realize it was I who healed them. I led them with cords of human kindness, with ties of love; I lifted the yoke from their neck and bent down to feed them.

What specifically impacts you about God's love for His children in this passage? What characteristics come to mind about God's authority?

Read Ephesians 6:4.

> Fathers, do not exasperate your children; instead, bring them up in the training and instruction of the Lord.

Applying this to your upbringing, how would you rate your parents' discipline?

2. Parental Faithfulness

We all know, intellectually, that God is ever faithful and that He will never leave us nor forsake us. At the same time, we often shrink from trusting Him. Childhood memories of broken promises or abandonment often are at the root of this distrust. Perhaps due to death or divorce you were physically separated from one or both of your parents. Or maybe you remember specific instances of loneliness. When we were young, we assumed everything Mom and Dad did was right. We certainly did not understand their humanness as we have the capability to do now as adults.

Donna is a mature, influential leader in my church in San Diego. However, she recently communicated her hardship with trusting God. It was an issue she had to resolve if she was going to grow as a Christian. As we talked one evening, she shared a vivid memory of when she was seven years old. Her father had abandoned the family but had contacted them later, and set up a date to spend time with Donna. She put on her best clothes and waited in the front yard for Dad to come. There was enormous anticipation on her part. Unfortunately, as you could probably guess, Donna waited, and waited, . . . and waited. Hours passed. Dad never did show up.

While Donna was very careful not to blame her dad for her present distrust, this was clearly a situation that needed to be released, forgiven, and dealt with.

THINK IT OVER/WRITE IT DOWN . . .

Read the following passages:
Hebrews 13:5

> Keep your lives free from the love of money and be content with what you have, because God has said, "Never will I leave you; never will I forsake you."

Matthew 28:20

> . . . and teaching them to obey everything I have commanded you. And surely I am with you always, to the very end of the age.

John 10:10

> The thief comes only to steal and kill and destroy; I have come that they may have life, and have it to the full.

2 Timothy 2:13

> . . . if we are faithless, he will remain faithful, for he cannot disown himself.

These are all wonderful promises from God. While it is not fair to compare your earthly parents to your Heavenly Father, it is beneficial to look at your parents' faithfulness to you and determine whether it tended to be inconsistent and unpredictable. Is there a specific time that you remember feeling lonely because of your parents' absence?

3. Parental Generosity

Parental generosity has to do with valuing people versus things. In our homes filled with valuable objects, antiques and other treasures, we all heard the words "don't touch that," or "leave that alone," or "put your hands in your pockets so you don't break anything" (my personal favorite). What becomes woven into our minds is the subtle concept that these things are more valuable than we are. This is especially true when the simple words "I love you" were not heard often enough.

God, however, is by nature generous. Just look around you at the creation that is His. He has lavished us with a beautifully abundant earth and He invites us to "taste and see that the Lord is good" (Psalm 34:8).

THINK IT OVER/WRITE IT DOWN . . .

Psalm 37:3–5 speaks of God's generosity.

> Trust in the Lord and do good; dwell in the land and enjoy safe pasture. Delight yourself in the Lord and he will give you the desires of your heart. Commit your way to the Lord; trust in him and he will do this.

Consider whether your upbringing was one that tended more toward God's generosity or the "don't touch" philosophy. Jot down your conclusions.

4. Parental Affection

As boys, this is often an area where our parents, especially our fathers, came up short. "Don't cry, son; boys don't cry" firmly establishes in us that emotion is not something to be exhibited. Many of us never experienced any display of physical affection at all. It just wasn't the "manly," brawny thing to do. God, in Jesus Christ, is not like that at all. He feels our hurts, He rejoices in our triumphs. His capacity for feeling is so much greater than ours because He knows suffering and rejection in a way no other man will ever have to experience.

All of us require affection. Man has identified diseases in babies who have not received enough physical affection during their first two years. In their book *The Blessing*, Gary Smalley and John Trent speak of giving "the blessing" to those near us. The blessing consists of five elements:

- Meaningful touch
- The spoken word
- Expressions of high value
- Description of a special future
- Application of genuine commitment[2]

Todd was just five years old when he decided he didn't want to be left alone in the dark at bedtime. He argued with his mom that he needed her next to him through the night. When she reminded him that God was always with him, Todd responded, "I know that, Mom. But I need someone with skin on them."

God's affection was intended to be exhibited through families. When it is absent, we tend to seek it from unhealthy sources. God is calling us back to health in our relationship to family and to Himself.

THINK IT OVER/WRITE IT DOWN . . .

On a scale of one to ten, how well do you exhibit emotion? "One" indicates little to no outward emotion and "ten" indicates you are completely free to express emotion.

1 2 3 4 5 6 7 8 9 10

How has this ability helped or hurt your relationship with God and others?

5. Parental Acceptance

We live in "Performance City." All around us are people urging us to do better, to climb higher, "to boldly go where no man has gone before." As kids, we received praise for performance from the day we were born, from potty training through adolescence. Making the grade, making the team, or making the money put pressures on us that seemed overwhelming. It was easy for us to translate that performance into "If I can just do this (or do it better/best) then I will be loved." While this may describe much or part of your time spent growing up, God's love is unconditional toward us. There are no strings attached. We are loved because of our position (as children), not our performance (as workers).

Dan and Maura had been married fourteen years. They had three children and a nice, suburban lifestyle. Maura spoke with me a year and a half ago, however, and hinted that Dan was becoming more and more impatient with her as time passed. I didn't think a whole lot about it until I learned they had begun seeing a counselor as a result. When I spoke to Dan, I asked if their marriage and family life were improving. He grew quiet and stared at the floor. After a moment, he looked up at me and shook his head. Tears filled his eyes as he said, "Tim, I am so filled with anger and bitterness, I don't know what to do. It's not Maura's fault, or the kids'—but I know I'm taking it out on them and I hate myself for it."

I probed gently for the cause. It didn't surprise me to discover the following elements to Dan's predicament:

- He was in a performance trap at work that reminded him of his home life when growing up.
- His parents' expectations were extremely high, and he was holding that same unrealistic standard over his own wife and kids.
- He had told himself that whenever he got married, he was *not* going to be like his dad—which is just the kind of focus that often causes sons to be *exactly* like their dad.
- The symptoms that showed up after fourteen years of marriage were identical to what happened after the same period of time in his parents' marriage.

We prayed together, but two weeks later Maura could stand it no longer. She asked him to leave indefinitely.

The good news is, Dan responded well. He decided to take initiative and confront the issue of his identity and security. He joined a small group of men who were studying how to become spiritual leaders in their home. It was remarkable to see God's healing hand so visibly on Dan during the next three to four months.

By the way, Dan and Maura are back together.

THINK IT OVER/WRITE IT DOWN . . .

Read Psalm 46:10.

> Be still, and know that I am God; I will be exalted among the nations, I will be exalted in the earth.

Read Zephaniah 3:17.

> The Lord your God is with you, he is mighty to save. He will take great delight in you, he will quiet you with his love, he will rejoice over you with singing.

Do you feel secure? Rejoiced over? Resting in His love? Or do you feel like you're still not measuring up? That there is always something more you must be doing? How does this affect your relationships with those who are close to you?

Do you have a difficult time simply receiving love, without immediately trying to turn around and do something to be worthy of it? Jot down your thoughts below.

Overcoming the Barriers

It is not my intent to convince you that your parents are "bad" people. Quite the contrary. One of the purposes of this section is to begin healing hurts that are already present. Until the hurts are revealed, healing cannot take place. There are no perfect people (or parents) in this world. All of us have failed others in relationships—parental or otherwise. All of us have suffered to some extent due to these failures. What is critically important is that we all come to a correct understanding of who God really is.

My concern is that we may stop short of this. It will do no good to dig up old memories or hurts if we do nothing about them. Let's not just fix the blame—let's fix the problem. The only good that can come from dealing with a hurtful past is to address the issues and become whole. Hurts often produce character flaws, and character flaws often prevent healthy spiritual leadership.

Emotional wholeness and healing are not hard to understand. They simply involve applying God's truth and grace to unresolved issues. As a result we can go forward, not in denial but in honesty. It is only then that we will be on the road to healthy leadership.

Steps to Breaking Hurt and Bitterness

If you have spotted a character flaw or trait that is weak because of an incorrect picture of God given you by a parent/authority, the following process might prove helpful to you. It is a list of steps for breaking hurt and bitterness. I suggest you go through each step with your partner.

1. **Recall:** Ask God to help you list events that caused hurt, bitterness, or the inability to respond to Him correctly.
2. **Reconstruct:** Ask God to reveal things *you've* done to hurt others—and Him.
3. **Release:** Ask forgiveness of God and the individuals involved.
4. **Request:** Ask the Holy Spirit to help you forgive and heal memories. Ask Him to enable you to do what is right.
5. **Renounce:** Refuse any bitterness; destroy "mental files."
6. **Return:** Get involved again in ministry in the lives of people.

Insights for Change

- *Remember,* this is a process. The outline above has no specified time frame.
- Be honest and open with your partner through this process. Even if you are not going through these steps

with her, she needs to be aware and praying. Openness fosters intimacy.

- These are not magical steps. The Holy Spirit is the healer, not the steps themselves. Trust in God. His love and grace will accomplish the work your will has begun.

Developing a Lifestyle

- Ask God to reveal any unresolved hurts or hindrances that detract from your ability to be the spiritual leader He wants you to be. Spend quiet time listening to anything God has to say.
- Memorize Hosea 11:1–4.

> When Israel was a child, I loved him, and out of Egypt I called my son. But the more I called Israel, the further they went from me. They sacrificed to the Baals and they burned incense to images. It was I who taught Ephraim to walk, taking them by the arms; but they did not realize it was I who healed them. I led them with cords of human kindness, with ties of love; I lifted the yoke from their neck and bent down to feed them.

- Pray with your partner concerning the barriers that prevent or hinder you from being an effective spiritual leader.

DOMESTIC CHORES
TOOLS
BIBLE

5

The Spiritual Leader as a Model

The private side of our lives is in reality what we model for those nearest us.

My wife and I have lived in our present home for about six years. Interestingly, it took us three years before we ever got around to putting in a back yard lawn. We just seemed to be content with dirt clods and tumbleweeds. It looked awful. The front yard was a different story—it was immaculate, with nice, colorful flowers. You would've thought I had a green thumb.

So what was the difference? That's simple. Our front yard was the public side of our property. People drove by it daily. Consequently, we were motivated to make it look good. The back yard, however, had a six-foot-high fence around it. No one ever saw it. One day, as I stood on our back patio viewing the pitiful-looking piece of real estate, the Lord impressed me with a profound truth: I was treating my life the same way I treated my lawn. The public side of my life appeared wonderful—I looked right, talked right, and acted right. But the private side of my life (my character, my motives, my thoughts—those things that we model unknowingly) never received enough attention. After all, I figured, no one notices or applauds invisible qualities like that. People don't keep score there . . . do they?

Unfortunately, I believe this is the dilemma of our generation. We live in a nation of leaders (even presumed spiritual leaders) who've failed to give attention to the private side of their lives. Sadly, this private side is in reality what we model for those nearest us. It doesn't take long for others to see through the veneer of wit and charisma and notice what kind of example really exists. Jesus said, "Out of the good treasure (deposit) of a good man's heart he brings forth good things" (Matthew 12:35, NASB). This works negatively, too. It's the "Acts 3 Principle." Do you remember Peter's words in Acts 3, when he was asked for money by the lame man? He said, "Silver and gold have I none, but what I do have—I can give to you." It's simple: We can only pass on to others what we possess ourselves.

This chapter will focus on the primary task of a spiritual leader: your role as a "model," one who exemplifies a life (and character) worth patterning after. In short, we are talking about an example of Christlikeness. Isn't this what the apostle Paul was speaking of when he said, "Follow me as I follow Christ" (1 Corinthians 11:1, NASB)?

Fortunately, being an example will not cause you to look like my cartoon character at the beginning of this chapter. However, there is more to modeling than what may appear on the surface.

Why You Must Be the Model

I frequently run into men who have accepted that they must set a good example, but are not convinced that this really makes the difference. It's the father who attempts to teach his son honesty, but instructs him to lie to a phone-caller by saying he is gone; or the dad who lectures to his kids on commitment, while he and their mother are in the divorce process; or the father who tries to instill in his kids how evil drugs are, while they watch him drink a couple of beers during Monday Night Football.

The principle underlying your need to set a good example is this:

> People don't do what they hear . . .
> *they do what they see.*

Note some unrelated but revealing survey results:

STATISTIC: The percentage of children who stay involved in church and Sunday school varies depending on the parental example. According to the Indianapolis Tech *Challenge* newsletter:

- 72 percent if both parents attend church and Sunday school
- 52 percent if only the father attends
- 15 percent if only the mother attends
- 5 percent if neither of them attend

What does this say to us as spiritual leaders? The *Challenge* article continues:

> In the 1940s the top offenses committed by public school students were talking, chewing gum, making noises, running in the halls, getting out of turn in line, wearing improper clothing, and not putting paper in the wastebasket.
>
> In 1982, the top offenses had changed. They had become rape, robbery, assault, burglary, arson, bombing, murder, and suicide.
>
> The behavior of children changed dramatically in the forty years separating those findings. Why? "Today's teenagers live in a different world from the one you remember. The nuclear family has exploded. Dr. Spock has given way to Dr. Ruth. A million hours of television have madc kids talk like valley girls, dress like rock stars, and think like game show contestants."[1]

Another perspective:

> Several years ago, the University of California tested fifth and sixth graders to determine what caused them the highest degree of sadness, anxiety, and depression. The top answers? Having parents separate or divorce, having parents argue with one another, and having parents who didn't spend time with them.[2]

My question is, if we don't model character in the home, where will our families find it?

STATISTIC: A few years ago our church college/career department conducted a survey among students at San Diego State University. The number one response to what is missing in America, according to university students, was that *there are no more models to follow.*

Clearly, during the last twenty-five years, young people have discarded political leaders as models to imitate. Also, fewer are able to spot good character in professional athletes today than twenty-five years ago. What we often see instead is selfishness and greed, and the need for arbitrators to negotiate multi-million dollar contracts. What's more, during the last decade, several religious broadcasters and televangelists have proven they have little inside that's worth patterning after. Yet they are in the spotlight; they are the visible ones whom everyone sees. So, how did they get into that spotlight if they weren't solid enough to handle adolescent temptation? The answer is the same. It's the dilemma of public versus private life: They possessed enough charisma to perform, but not enough character to empower. Though our lifestyle isn't together, our lip service continues—the show must go on!

Do you remember the space shuttle *Challenger* and the horrible explosion that took seven lives in 1986? Soon after the accident, reporters discovered that NASA quality control workers had warned other departments that some areas of the spacecraft were in need of more work before the flight.

But alas, production was paramount. Again, the show must go on. And we paid dearly for it.

The bottom line is obvious. We must give priority attention to the private, inner areas of our lives, for they are surely what we will model and reproduce in those closest to us.

What You Must Model

You may feel that you have quite a task ahead of you in becoming an example. After all, none of us is perfect and no one is purely Christlike. So how do we keep from getting overwhelmed? Where do we begin in our example?

I frequently hear the question put this way: "Since I cannot be perfect at everything, what are the essentials that I must model for my partner and family?" Or, if you are single: "What are the essentials that those who are closest to me are watching for?" That's a good question. I believe these are the five essential categories:

Quality:	**Your family will ask:**
Attitude	Does he demonstrate a positive, godly attitude?
Time with God	Does he demonstrate submission through prayer?
Conversation	How disciplined is his conversation?
Time with Family	Are we a priority investment in his life?
Associates	With whom does he spend outside time?

THINK IT OVER/WRITE IT DOWN . . .

How are you doing at modeling these? Which quality is your strongest? Which is your weakest?

Have you been able to see how your failure to model these has affected those nearest you? How has it?

My college chaplain was a man by the name of Bob Stamps. One afternoon, Bob returned home from the campus to spend a little time with his wife and two preschool children. When he didn't see his wife in the house, he assumed they were all out on an errand. Then Bob heard a noise that often spells trouble: the sound of giggles coming from the back bedroom. It was his kids, and he could tell they were up to no good. He raced back to find them, each with a pair of scissors, giving each other haircuts. It was horrible. Both had snipped their hair down to the scalp, leaving no bangs at all over their foreheads. Bob was stunned, but his fatherly instincts soon took over. He removed the scissors from the vicinity, then took his oldest son and prepared to give him a spanking. Just as Bob had turned his little boy across his knee, the boy looked at him and cried, "But daddy, we were only trying to be like you!" He paused. You see, Bob is bald.

You can probably guess that those kids never got that spanking. After all, how could a father punish a child for trying to imitate him?

That is what spiritual leadership is about—understanding that you are being imitated as you imitate God, in Christ. Children almost always look like their parents.

Incarnational Leadership

Let's look for a moment at both the dilemma and the solution involved in modeling. As I've mentioned, leadership is first what you *are* before it is something you *do*. It is "being before doing." One counselor said that the chief problem in many cases is that we've become "human-doings" before we are human beings. However, you can only really model something when it has become a part of your life. That's what we mean by incarnational leadership.

Below is a diagram first developed for church leaders by Dr. John Maxwell. In it he illustrates the need to move from the left column (What I Am) toward the right column (Result) via the middle column (What I Do). But because we are so preoccupied with results, performance and production, we're often tempted to move from right to left.

WHAT I AM	WHAT I DO	RESULT
Humble	Rely on God	Power
Convictional	Sacrifice	Commitment
People lover	Give	Security
Visionary	Set goals	High morals

For instance, we may be so consumed with desiring to see power in our lives (Result column), that we move leftward and try feverishly to rely on God since that's what produces a powerful life. Most of the time our attempts are done in our own strength and are short-lived. We become frustrated.

God is saying to us, however, "Why don't you simply *become* humble? Why not develop humility in your 'being' —then you will naturally rely on Me, and the result will be power."

The same is true with commitment. We long to see commitment results in the lives of our family and particularly our children. So we "try" to sacrifice in an attempt to show them how it's done. Again, it's usually short-lived and we burn out. God responds, "Develop a convictional character, then you will naturally sacrifice on issues on which you possess convictions, and the result will be commitment in those who follow you."

An illustration of what can happen when we approach this issue incorrectly comes from my own church family. We have always prized our music department. Consequently, we have taken young singers who've displayed talent, put them on the platform with a microphone, and cheered "Sing!" Unfortunately, we have not given equal time to ensure that they've been spiritually and emotionally ready for the many musical productions in which they have performed. We have rewarded the results and often neglected the character development. And those young musicians become confused, because they hear the applause after a performance and frequently mistake this applause of the people for the blessing of God.

I recently spoke with one twenty-six-year-old man who fit that category. He still has never developed spiritually because of the reversed emphasis on "doing" before "being." He is a spiritual mess.

THINK IT OVER/WRITE IT DOWN . . .

Note how we tend to move from right to left in the diagram on page 77, rather than vice versa. Why do you think this is?

What steps must you take to attain the qualities listed on the left side of the diagram?

Your Network

You can tell a lot about yourself and your lifestyle by identifying those who compose your "network." Complete the following diagram, developed by author Keith Drury, inserting the names of people who affect the direction of your life. By seeing how your life is invested, and who influences you, you will better know what adjustments will be necessary.

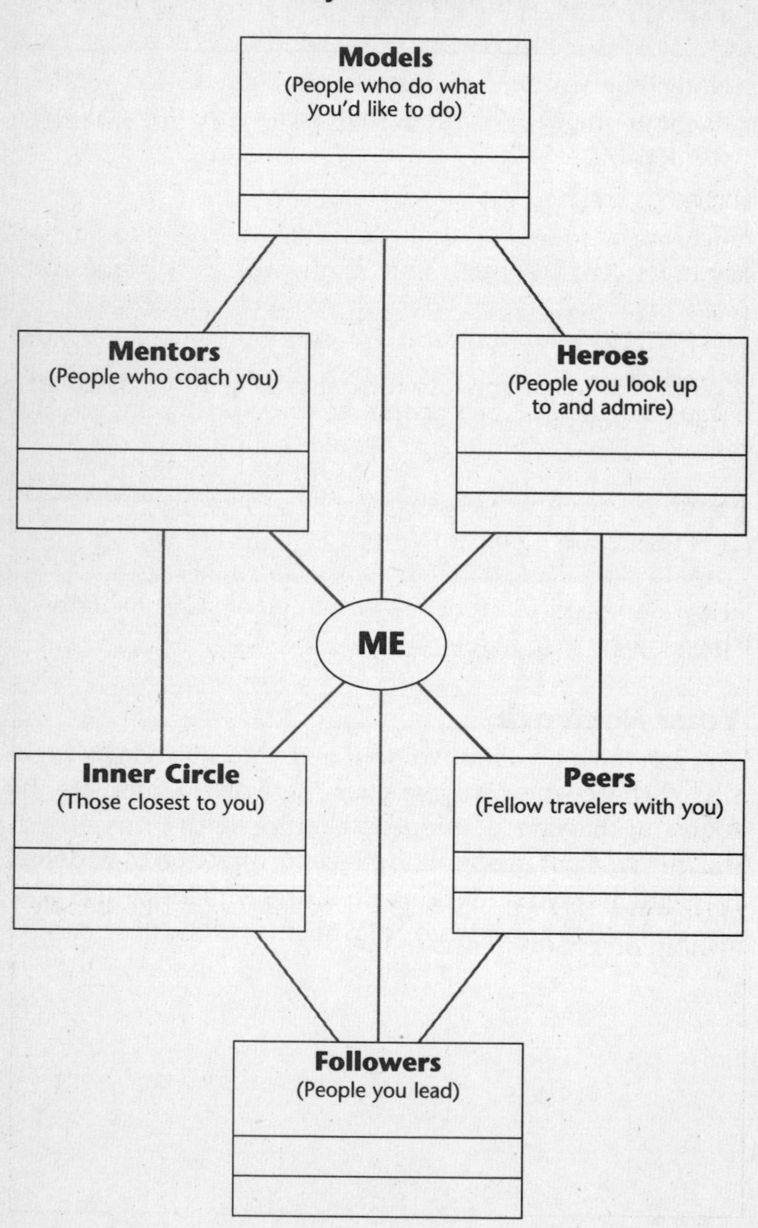
My Network
Models
(People who do what you'd like to do)
Mentors
(People who coach you)
Heroes
(People you look up to and admire)
ME
Inner Circle
(Those closest to you)
Peers
(Fellow travelers with you)
Followers
(People you lead)

- Note those who are your models, mentors and heroes.
- Note those with whom your family sees you spending time.
- Note those who appear to have priority in your life.

Interpreting Your Influence

Once you've identified the traits that you must model, the key ingredient to understand is influence. Think about it: *Leadership is influence.*

This is the greatest one-word definition for what it means to lead. If this is true, then all of us lead to some degree, because all of us have people whom we influence. Let's discuss this idea of influence for a moment.

THINK IT OVER/WRITE IT DOWN . . .

How do you gain influence in the life of another? (How have others gained it in your life?)

List some biblical characters who proved to be people whom others wanted to follow.

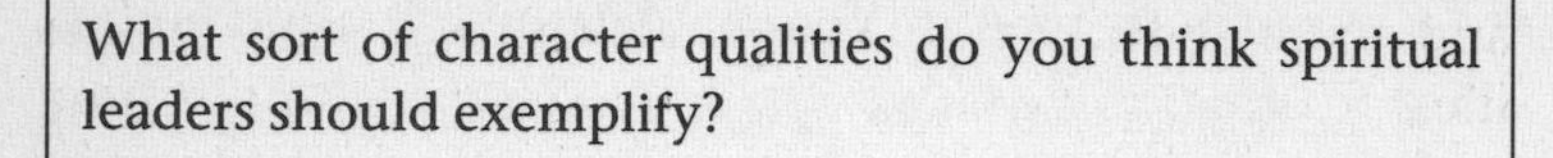

What sort of character qualities do you think spiritual leaders should exemplify?

What qualities do you feel you model well to your partner?

Is it difficult for you to model spiritual leadership at your workplace? Why or why not?

The Price of Spiritual Leadership

All this modeling will require sacrifice on your part. There is a definite price to pay. Let's conclude this chapter by looking at a simple acrostic using the word "PRICE" that will serve as a reminder of the cost of modeling spiritual leadership.

P – *Priorities*

This earmarks a spiritual model. Your agenda reflects your priorities. Someone once said, "Show me a man's checkbook and his calendar and I'll tell you what's most valued in his life." It's true. It shows up first in our home with our time and treasure. John Wesley was once asked if a particular man with whom he'd just become acquainted was a Christian. Wesley responded, "I don't know, I haven't asked his wife yet."

I'm sure you remember the pop song during the 1970s entitled "The Cat's In the Cradle." The lyrics vividly describe the relationship between a father and his young son growing up. The son continually requests time with his dad but never seems to get it. Nevertheless, the boy idolizes his dad and promises, "I'm going to be like you, Dad" (when I grow up). As the song ends, the father is now wanting time with his son but is unable to get it, and he concludes with remorse: "My boy has become just like me." Ouch. The sad truth is, we not only *reflect* our priorities with our very lives, but we *reproduce* our priorities within those nearest us.

Where do you make the greatest investments of your time and energy: home? job? church? friendships?

How do your time investments reflect what's important to you?

R – *Risk Taking*

As a spiritual leader, you're willing to step out first. You are vulnerable, transparent, and honest at all costs. You exemplify security in the Lord.

I'm afraid I haven't always done well in this category. Just before I met my wife, Pam, I was involved in a relationship that wasn't too healthy. It was a sort of love-hate, teeter-totter relationship that swung to extremes and involved jealousy and insecurity. I'm certain there was a lot of immaturity on my part, too. I was a poor model of the kind of stability and vulnerability required for a deep, healthy commitment. I was not a risk taker. I was too busy getting my own needs met to give anything away. It was messy; we fought, and eventually the relationship crumbled. I've since learned that being a risk taker requires my becoming a secure person in the Lord.

How well do you risk your reputation, image and faith through vulnerability, transparency and honesty?

Why is it difficult to take risks among friends? At your workplace? In your church?

I – *Initiative*

Spiritual leaders are initiators. They are hosts, not guests, in their relationships. In the same way that you invite a friend into your home and see to his comfort when he visits, so does a spiritual leader take initiative to host conversations and relationships in which he's involved. This, I am afraid, will take effort—it is not natural for most men. Elisabeth Elliot writes:

> Women are always tempted to be initiators. We like to get things done. We want to talk about situations and feelings, get it all out in the open, deal with it. It appears to us that men often ignore and evade issues, sweep things under the rug, forget about them, get on with projects, business, pleasures, sports, eat a big steak, turn on the television, roll over, and go to sleep. Women respond to this tendency by insisting on confrontation, communication, showdown. If we can't dragoon our men into that, we nag, we plead, we get attention by tears, silence, or withholding warmth and intimacy. We have a large bag of tricks.
>
> C.S. Lewis's vision of purgatory was a place where milk was always boiling over, crockery smashing, and toast burning. The lesson assigned to the men was to do something about it. The lesson for the women was to do nothing.[3]

Clearly, initiative will require a conscious effort on our part.

Do you tend to be a host or a guest in conversations with people?

C – *Character*

A spiritual leader, as I have mentioned, develops himself on the inside first. He is convinced that his personal, private disciplines done when no one is watching will pay off eventually, when many may be watching. He knows that character, or lack of it, really can be seen.

We often hide behind weak excuses for our lack of character. During the 1980s, Dr. Ruth Westheimer told us that sex was to be freely expressed, and that it wasn't natural for us to curb or restrain our sexual impulses. After all, animals don't. Ironically, while Dr. Ruth was promoting this belief all over America, several university students from communist China were asked on television about their sexual experience. Each of the students responded that they'd never had sex before. When asked why not, each explained that they weren't married yet. And when the American interviewer asked, "Why would you not have sex before you were married?" the students replied almost in unison: "Because it's wrong." Isn't it sad that we often see strength of character exhibited in a godless country more so than in America?

What personal disciplines are reflected in your life?

Where is it most difficult for you to exercise discipline: home? work? the church? Why?

E – *Eagerness*

A spiritual leader is a teachable person with a hungry mind. He is always ready to grow and is as enthusiastic as a little child about following Christ. True spiritual leaders never stop growing, and maintain a humble spirit, openly depending upon God.

I believe this kind of attitude is not only blessed by God, but essential for our family and followers to see. It helps remove us from the impossible pedestal of "I Have Arrived" and models a receptive heart to those who learn by watching you.

How are you modeling eagerness and teachability?

Do you model an "eager heart" among your friends? Why or why not?

Developing a Lifestyle

- Memorize Philippians 2:5–11.

  Your attitude should be the same as that of Christ Jesus: Who, being in very nature God, did not consider equality with God something to be grasped, but made himself nothing, taking the very nature of a servant, being made in human

> likeness. And being found in appearance as a man, he humbled himself and became obedient to death—even death on a cross! Therefore God exalted him to the highest place and gave him the name that is above every name, that at the name of Jesus every knee should bow, in heaven and on earth and under the earth, and every tongue confess that Jesus Christ is Lord, to the glory of God the Father.

- Look at your network diagram. Choose one of your mentors or models and have a meal with him. Ask what has made him effective in the areas he models for you.
- Pick a leader in the Bible. Read the Scripture that outlines his biography, and list the characteristics that made him such an effective and influential example.
- Ask your partner what you model best in your life. (If you need an area to start with, look again at the P-R-I-C-E of leadership.)

6

The Spiritual Leader as a Minister

No matter what career you have chosen to provide your income, Jesus said all leaders are to be ministers.

Authority and submission have always been difficult issues for my generation. In our disdain of "kissing up" to authority structures, we have butted heads with the powers that be on numerous occasions.

During a cold, dark evening off the Atlantic seacoast, a captain noticed the lights of another ocean vessel directly in his ship's path. He quickly sent a message requesting that this vessel change its course 10 degrees south. A reply came back promptly, "Change *your* course 10 degrees north." This angered the captain, so he added a little "punch" to his next request, "Change your course 10 degrees south—this is Captain John C. Smith." Back came the response, "Change your course 10 degrees north—this is seaman third class James Johnson." Now the captain was livid. No one had ever been so insubordinate to his authority. He decided to send what he thought was an irrefutable imperative: "Change your course 10 degrees south. I am a battleship." Without any hesitation, the reply came back: "Change your course 10 degrees north—I am a lighthouse!"

This humorous little episode serves as a good platform for the subject of this chapter. Jesus told us that, as leaders, we are faced with an interesting challenge. It is not that of pressing others into submission. Rather, it is the paradox of submitting ourselves to serving those who follow us. Remember the axiom, "We lead by serving; we serve by leading." The past four chapters have examined some of the roles of the spiritual leader as well as our call to model what we expect our partner, friends, co-workers, and family to be. Now we will look at the spiritual leader as a "minister."

Think about this statement for just a moment: *You are a minister!* No matter what career you have chosen to provide your income, Jesus said all leaders are to be ministers (Matthew 20:26, KJV). This is your "vocation." (The word "vocation" incidentally, is taken from the word "vocal" or "calling.") You have been "ordained" already (John 15:16, KJV), and the apostle Paul commands us to walk worthy of this ministry vocation (Ephesians 4:1).

THINK IT OVER/WRITE IT DOWN . . .

As a spiritual leader in your relationships, you are called to *minister* to your partner. What sort of images does this evoke? Write down some words that come to mind.

On a scale of 1 to 10 (with 10 being the most effective), circle the number that reflects how effective a minister you are to your partner, friends, and co-workers:

1 2 3 4 5 6 7 8 9 10

Why did you circle this number?

If it's any consolation, remember that the toughest area for men to serve and minister is right in their own home. It is generally easier for us to "serve" our colleagues in business and at church than it is to serve the one with whom we chose to spend the rest of our life.

As a pastor, I am ashamed to admit my shortcomings in this area. Late one evening about four years ago, I returned home from a hard day of "ministry" at the church office. I felt fairly good about the strategic way I had invested my time that week. My ministry was growing numerically. Unfortunately, this occupied most of my thinking.

As I entered through the garage door, Pam wasn't there to greet me as she usually does. Although it was late, this surprised me. I walked into the bedroom to find that she had already gone to bed. When I leaned over her to see if she was asleep, I suddenly noticed her eyes were open and filled with tears. I was startled. My mind raced through its files, wondering if I had forgotten something significant or if she had experienced something traumatic or discouraging that day. I was clueless. So I whispered to her directly, "What's wrong?"

There was a pause. Then, looking up at me with painful eyes, she said gently, "Tim, you're doing such a great job caring for the people of the church. And I don't want to stand in the way of that. But . . . there is no ministry taking place here in our home at all. Right now, I feel alone and forgotten."

Those words shook me up. They were not any easier for her to say than they were for me to hear. I knew I had to make some changes. I had neglected, as a pastor, my number one parishioner.

Jesus Set the Pace

In Matthew 20:25–28, Jesus taught that the leader in a Christian relationship operates very differently from the non-Christian leader. The worldly leader exercises all sorts of rights in his life; the Christian (spiritual) leader becomes a servant. And servants aren't concerned with rights, but with responsibilities.

> Jesus called them together and said, "You know that the rulers of the Gentiles lord it over them, and their high officials exercise authority over them. Not so with you. Instead, whoever wants to become great among you must be your servant, and whoever wants to be first must be your slave—just as the Son of Man did not come to be served, but to serve, and to give his life as a ransom for many."

The following diagram illustrates this principle of servant leadership.

The Spiritual Leadership Triangle

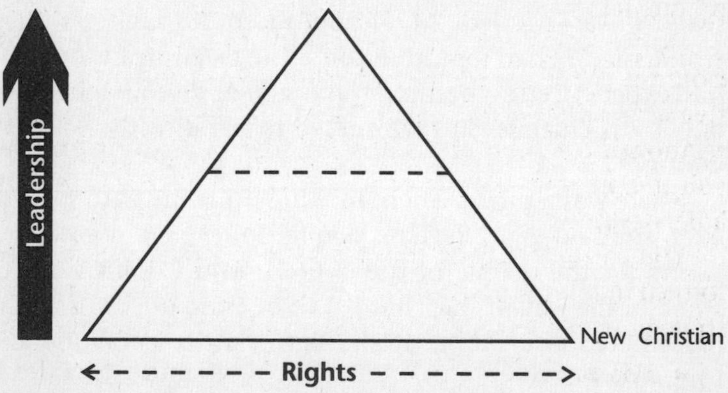

Leadership

New Christian

← – – – – – – – Rights – – – – – – – – →

As you move upward into higher levels of leadership, you are to surrender rights that were available to you as a new Christian. God allows a lot of behavioral freedom for babes in Christ. However, note the width of the dotted line further up the leadership triangle. It is substantially narrower and will continue to be so as leadership increases. The ultimate goal is to say with the apostle Paul, "I am a bond servant (slave) of the Lord Jesus Christ" (Romans 1:1). Paul lived at the top of the triangle. He knew that slaves give up their rights. They just serve.

Sadly, what has been modeled for us in the world, and even by some Christian leaders in the media, has been an inverted triangle. Their actions imply that leadership means we gain all sorts of options and rights: I can sleep with whomever I want; I can spend whatever money I want; I can drink whatever I wish, etc. Jesus simply said, "It is not so among you." Then He demonstrated this radical servant leadership.

The Foot Washing

Following His Last Supper with the disciples, Jesus took a towel and a bowl of water and washed their feet. A servant (or minister) would normally do this before a meal, but since no one had volunteered that evening, Jesus did so.

Do you recall the principle of the guest versus the host from the previous chapter? Jesus modeled taking the initiative as a host would. Again, He understood that in every relationship a guest and a host emerge, depending on who will *initiate* to make the other feel loved, secure, comfortable, or ministered to.

You can read about this grand foot washing Jesus performed in John 13 (NASB). The text is careful to point out the strategic elements of Jesus' ministry to His men that evening:

- **His motive.** Jesus' motive for serving the disciples is described in verse 1. Take note of it. The passage tells us Jesus "loved His own . . . He loved them to the end." A deep love had developed for those people the Father had entrusted to Him.

- **His security.** Jesus' security for serving is outlined in verses 3 and 4. He was able to give in a vulnerable, unorthodox, and profound manner—washing men's feet is certainly all of those—because He possessed this security: "Knowing that the Father had given all things into His hands, and that He had come forth from God and was going back to God, rose from supper . . . and washed their feet." Jesus knew who He was, where He'd come from, and where He was going.
- **His reasoning.** Why did Jesus do it? There was more to it than just the fact they had dirty feet. Jesus took on the house-servant's job description that evening to prove a point. He was teaching an object lesson to them, and to us, as leaders. Note what verses 12 through 15 say:

> And so, when He had washed their feet . . . He said to them, "Do you know what I have done to you? You call me Teacher and Lord, and you are right, for so I am. If I then, the Lord and the Teacher, washed your feet, you also ought to wash one another's feet. For I gave you an example that you also should do as I did to you."

THINK IT OVER/WRITE IT DOWN . . .

Jesus exemplified three attitudes in this text that are difficult for us as males (and as leaders) in our society. Note these attitudes, and consider the following questions.

Nothing to prove. Jesus didn't have to play any games, or construct any façades to prove something or to project Himself or His position. He was confident and secure in His person and purpose.

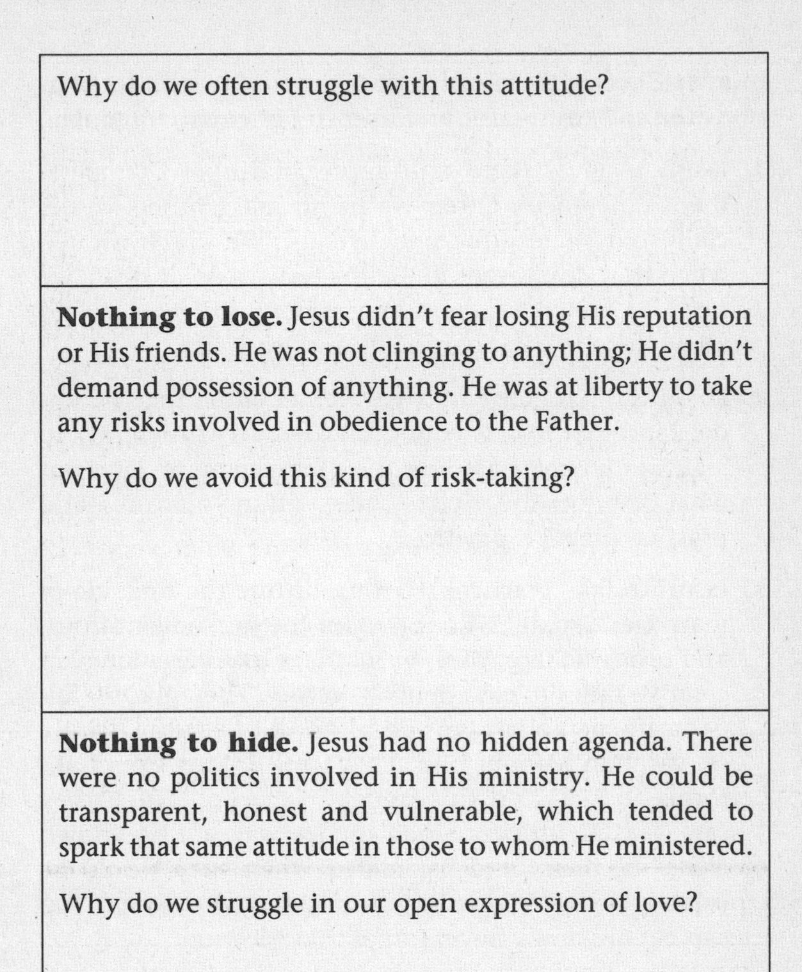

Why do we often struggle with this attitude?

Nothing to lose. Jesus didn't fear losing His reputation or His friends. He was not clinging to anything; He didn't demand possession of anything. He was at liberty to take any risks involved in obedience to the Father.

Why do we avoid this kind of risk-taking?

Nothing to hide. Jesus had no hidden agenda. There were no politics involved in His ministry. He could be transparent, honest and vulnerable, which tended to spark that same attitude in those to whom He ministered.

Why do we struggle in our open expression of love?

Pastor Bill Hybels recently offered three suggestions to couples as he addressed this subject at Willow Creek Community Church, just outside of Chicago. In order for relationships to be authentic and ministry oriented, we must:

1. Learn to understand and appreciate inborn temperament differences. Often we try to make others—especially our mates—become like us. We are frustrated when they don't react to life the way we do. Instead, we need to welcome the temperament differences and allow them to balance, polish, and teach us.

2. Learn the "language of love." It's essential that we understand that love is communicated very differently to and from people based on their temperament. Find out what best does the trick to those within your care—and practice, practice, practice!

3. Learn to take practical steps to nurture the fun side of marriage. Couples who maintain the fun, adventurous, and romantic facet of their marriage are ones who plan creative times to experience together. They purposefully create memories. One dad I know of sent his family on vacation without him. They were driving from California to Texas on this holiday excursion when they saw Dad hitchhiking along the freeway. He had flown ahead of them, and calculated when they would be driving by—and joined them in this unusual way. You can bet his family never forgot that vacation!

Meeting Your Partner's Needs

The primary task of a servant is to meet needs. Consequently, you can gauge how well you perform this function with your partner by asking yourself, "How effective am I at ministering to her needs?"

Your partner's primary needs fall into three basic categories: attention, affirmation and affection.

1. Attention

This involves stopping long enough to really notice her, to listen to her, and to develop a concern about what's important to her.

THINK IT OVER/WRITE IT DOWN . . .

How well have you done this in your relationship? Why or why not?

What are her main interests?

How could you better meet this need of attention?

2. Affirmation

This involves giving her "strokes," encouraging her strengths, and letting her know that she's valuable and that you believe in her.

THINK IT OVER/WRITE IT DOWN . . .

How well have you done this in your relationship? Why or why not?

What are her strengths?

How could you better meet this need of affirmation?

3. Affection

This involves open and candid display of love, finding creative and tangible ways to communicate your feelings, and yes—even showing a bit of romance.

THINK IT OVER/WRITE IT DOWN . . .

How well have you done this in your relationship? Why or why not?

What do you think communicates love and affection to her?

How could you better meet this need of affection?

In a Nutshell

Be alert to the following things you could do for your partner:

- Stop and listen to her.
- Show you care about what's important to her.
- Give her your undivided attention.
- Encourage her strengths.
- Ask her, "What communicates love to you?" Then do it!

I shudder to think of the times I have failed to communicate my wife's value through attention, affirmation and affection. What's more, the things that replaced her time and position in my life were often mundane and temporal. Though women may never express it, I wonder how many could have written the following piece to their husbands:

> I would rather be your morning paper,
> than the one who made you breakfast.
>
> I would rather be your secretary,
> than the one who never made eye contact last night.
>
> I would rather be your client,
> than the one who put your untouched supper in the refrigerator and went to bed.
>
> I would rather be your hunting dog,
> than the one who took the kids on vacation without you.
>
> I would rather be your pastor,
> than the one who never gets things done quite right.
>
> I would rather be your lawyer or accountant,
> than the one who knows more of Sesame Street than Wall Street.
>
> I would rather be your golf partner,
> than the one you always leave behind.

I would rather be thanked than ignored.

I would rather be touched than brushed aside.

I would rather be nurtured than stifled.

I would rather be your wife,
but I gave up on that long ago.

by Michael Hodgin[1]

Why Is This So Hard for Me?

As you think about your role as a minister, you may feel that this is a difficult function to perform. If so, there are probably several reasons for this. Note the following and see if you can identify any of these in your life:

- **Fear:** We fear being a failure as the godly leader we're supposed to be.
- **Low self-esteem:** We're not secure enough to give of ourselves.
- **Embarrassment:** We avoid being vulnerable; what if they don't respond?
- **Not enough time:** We have a stressed and busy schedule.
- **Shallowness:** We're good at trivia but not at meaningful expression.
- **Intellectualization:** We analyze and scrutinize the relationship from the outside.
- **Discernment:** We're out of touch with both her feelings and ours.
- **Image:** To serve and express love seems feminine—"big boys" don't do that.

THINK IT OVER/WRITE IT DOWN . . .

Which ones do you battle with in your life?

Why do you think you do?

Jot down some action steps you can take to overcome these.

Cowboys and Playboys

Sociologist Jack Balswick writes:

> One of the true tragedies of American life is the fact that so many American men—perhaps a majority—choke on the words, "I love you."
>
> He is like the old Vermonter, married forty years, who remarked, "I love my wife so much, sometimes I can hardly keep from telling her so."[2]

Why is expression difficult? Because expressions of love and affection are generally stereotyped as feminine behavior. Even from the media, we have developed "images" and "heroes" that produce inexpressive males. For the sake of this study we will call those masculine images the "cowboys" and the "playboys."

The Cowboy

Historically the U.S. has admired the cowboy as a symbol of masculinity. This is the "John Wayne" type who feels more comfortable around his horse than around his girl. He does like women, but at the right time and in the right place—which he chooses. And always with his horse (or car) parked directly outside, on which he will ride away to his more important business in "Marlboro Country."

His image is . . .

- the rugged type
- resilient
- "he-man"
- resourceful
- strong
- courteous but reserved

The Playboy

This image is portrayed more as the "James Bond" type. Like the cowboy, he is resourceful and shrewd and interacts with his girlfriend with a certain detachment. This is simply expressed as "playing it cool." Bond is more of a "Don Juan," and departs from the cowboy image in that he is nonfeeling. Where John Wayne does have feelings (however unwilling to show them) and puts women on a pedestal, James Bond rejects women as women, treating them as consumer commodities.

His image is . . .

- lover, but emotionally uninvolved
- cunning

- avoids emotional attachment
- self-sufficient
- manipulator
- has his own agenda

The conclusion then is:

The Cowboy = the inexpressive feeling man

The Playboy = the inexpressive nonfeeling man

THINK IT OVER/WRITE IT DOWN . . .

You just saw two lists describing the cowboy and playboy images. Hopefully, you fit neither of these stereotypes. But if you err in one direction, which side would you resemble more (circle one)?

The Cowboy or The Playboy

Why is this?

How would you describe your ability or inability to express love, ministry, and servanthood to your partner?

Some Final Steps

In addition to the earlier suggestions in this chapter, here are some final action steps you can take to be a better minister to your partner:

1. Build trust through communication.
2. Plan time to talk.
3. Be an active listener by asking questions.
4. Ask forgiveness for your shortcomings.
5. Look for things you can do to help her.
6. Learn to open up and express feelings.

Developing a Lifestyle

- Ask your partner what communicates love to her. Discuss this with her; plan to do something about it.
- Memorize Matthew 20:25–28.

  > Jesus called them together and said, "You know that the rulers of the Gentiles lord it over them, and their high officials exercise authority over them. Not so with you. Instead, whoever wants to become great among you must be your servant, and whoever wants to be first must be your slave—just as the Son of Man did not come to be served, but to serve, and to give his life as a ransom for many."

- Interview a husband who demonstrates ministry to his wife; ask him what he does and why.

OK, KIDS-- LISTEN UP, NOW.
I'M THE HEAD OF THIS HOUSE,
AND WHAT I SAY, GOES!
YOU GOT THAT, KIDS? ...KIDS?
M
ELVIS

7

The Spiritual Leader as a Mentor

As a mentor you must be committed to three things: a person, a process, and a purpose.

Sociologists tell us that the most introverted of persons will influence an average of 10,000 other people during his lifetime. That is a remarkable statistic to me.

If introverted, withdrawn, non-leadership-type individuals influence that many other people, imagine what kind of influence you and I might exercise who aspire to leadership! Influence is what leadership is all about. Remember, it's the simplest one-word definition of leadership. In this chapter, we will discuss how we can effectively influence those under our care through the practice of "mentoring."

Mentoring, like modeling and ministering, is yet another role of the spiritual leader. It has become a popular subject today in our often detached and uncommitted culture. Authors and lecturers on leadership frequently suggest that everyone find a mentor and a protegé (someone to guide them and someone who needs their guidance) as they progress through the stages of life. But just what does it mean to mentor? And how does this idea of mentoring fit into our homes and churches? What kind of commitment and ability are required of us, if God is indeed calling us to mentor our spouses, friends and children? Can we really do it?

What Is a Mentor, Anyway?

In our context, a mentor is one who assumes responsibility for the *development* of his partner or family. The key term is "development." The spiritual mentor is called to be a:

- Guide
- Encourager
- Resource
- Evaluator
- Provider

When I think of the term "mentor," it conjures up images of a tradesman or craftsman developing a young apprentice in old England. Can you see it? Cobblestone streets, with horses and carriages; a shop off the main street where this craftsman works, all the while being observed by an up-and-coming young man who wants one day to own a shop of his own. The craftsman spends time explaining his work to the curious, onlooking apprentice; allowing him to try his hand at doing the work himself to gain the skill; then debriefing the young man at the close of the day. What a beautiful analogy for the spiritual leader.

Dr. Tony Campolo, in his book *Who Switched the Price Tags?*, reports the results of a survey of retired people living in their twilight years. In response to the question, "If you could live your life over again, what changes would you make?" they shared three common answers:

- I would reflect more. (I would take the time to stop and make sense of the journey I was on.)
- I would risk more. (I played it too safe. I would take more risks in the areas that count.)
- I would invest my life in areas that will outlive me. (I would try to leave a legacy behind me by investing in the lives of others.)[1]

All three answers are insightful, but note the third one again. That statement is the vision and fruit of a mentor. It is pouring your life, wisdom, skills and spirit into the life of another so that there is spiritual reproduction—life multiplication. Does this sound strangely biblical? If Jesus called us to "make disciples of all nations," might that best begin in our homes, and with those already in our sphere of influence? Parenting is the ultimate discipleship. Mentoring is the ultimate in spiritual leadership.

Perhaps the biblical illustration of the shepherd will effectively describe this role of a mentor. The shepherd is responsible for his sheep, for their well-being, food (growth), safety, direction, and ongoing life. He literally invests part of his life in the flock.

By analogy, I cannot think of a wiser investment of our time and energy than in the people God has placed right under our noses. They are eternal treasures, immortal souls with the potential of Jesus within them (John 14:12, 1 John 2:6). I believe we were designed for that kind of fulfilling, satisfying investment. A television interview reminded me of this some years ago. Just after the annual Rose Bowl Parade in Pasadena, California, a young float-builder was interviewed and asked whether he enjoyed constructing those huge, multifaceted floats each year. When he replied that he did, he was asked if he had considered doing it as a career. His response was a decisive "No," and then he explained why: "I could never imagine investing so much of myself into something that's thrown into the scrap pile within a matter of weeks." Great insight! How often do we sell ourselves short by investing so much in such insignificant, temporal, and trivial causes? As a spiritual leader, my wife, my daughter, and my church staff are ones in which I should be investing. They are the legacy I will leave behind.

Jonathan and David

Two young men who exhibit the kind of relationship conducive for mentoring are found in the book of 1 Samuel. These two individuals, Jonathan and David, are accountable to each other in their relationship, and as peers they find themselves mentoring each other during their lives. We see in them mutual submission, commitment to growth, and a deep, loving investment in the other—the kind that desires the very best for the other in light of the big picture. Note four qualities they possess—availability, dependability, vulnerability and responsibility—as seen in 1 Samuel 20. Get your Bible and let's make these discoveries together.

Availability (1 Samuel 20:1–4)

In these verses, David articulates the dangerous predicament he is in with Jonathan's own father, Saul. Note that Jonathan, even in his initial disbelief of David's danger, makes himself completely available to him in his crisis. He is at David's disposal. As mentors, we must be available, perceiving interruptions from our protegés as divine appointments. I shudder to think of how many signals I have given my wife and daughter that I was too busy for them. In the first part of this century a young boy was scarred for life by his parents as he grew up during World War I in Germany. His family, the Schicklewubers, had developed distorted priorities that left the boy emotionally alone and confused. He overheard his father talk about moving away one evening, and assumed that he would be abandoned. He decided then to toughen up and find refuge in things outside of love and family. The world has suffered much from that decision—for you and I know this young boy as Nazi dictator Adolf Hitler. I have to wonder how history might have been altered if young Adolf had had a godly mentor available to him.

What are two ways you could improve your availability to your partner/family or your friends/co-workers?

Dependability (1 Samuel 20:5–16)

Note in these verses that David and Jonathan enter into a trust, or a covenant, to do what is right and best for each other. These are not empty words they exchange. David's life is being threatened and both he and Jonathan vow to be dependable unto death to carry out God's will. This exchange reminds us all of the commitment necessary in a mentoring relationship. Trust and dependability are essential hand-in-glove qualities we must cultivate. I spoke with a woman recently who could not fathom a God who is trustworthy and faithful in both word and deed. The problem was simple. The three influential men in her life—her father, ex-husband, and present husband—had all failed to exhibit any form of dependability. She was now a loner with a lot of emotional walls in her life.

What are two ways you could improve your dependability toward your partner/family or your friends/co-workers?

Vulnerability (1 Samuel 20:17–33)

At this point in the text, Jonathan becomes absolutely vulnerable, and even risks his life and future position as king for David's sake. He is willing to be open and to gamble away his own comfort—and to go out on a limb for David's future. David is the only one who would gain from this vulnerability. In terms of position (royal status), Jonathan can only lose, or break even at best. But, you see, David is his priority. He is investing in the future of both his friend and his country.

As I have mentioned in earlier chapters, we struggle with vulnerability. We don't like giving up things that are ours, when only others benefit as a result. It just doesn't seem fair to shrewd, sophisticated adults, especially men. Maybe that's why Jesus said "become like little children" (Matthew 18:3). Susan was just five years old when her daddy told her to be home by 6 p.m. one evening. When she returned home late from her friend's house, he met her at the door and questioned why she wasn't on time. She said, "Daddy, I tried hard to be on time, but Tracy's doll broke and I had to stay longer." Her father paused, then questioned again, "Oh, and I suppose you were helping her put it back together?" Susan looked at her dad squarely and said, "No, I was helping her cry."

What are two ways you could improve your vulnerability with your partner/family or your friends/co-workers?

Responsibility (1 Samuel 20:34–42)

Finally, note that both Jonathan and David carry out what is right for everyone involved. They model responsibility when it would have been easier to take shortcuts. We clearly see the character and discipline needed in an effective mentor. It should be added that this kind of biblical responsibility is not only absent in much of our culture today, but is not even fostered. Our work is cut out for us. Irresponsibility is groomed on all levels from the home to the legal system in our courtrooms. A few years go in Los Angeles a drunk driver was weaving his way down a city street when he drove his car up onto the curb, hitting a gentleman inside a phone booth. The phone booth was turned on its side when the paramedics arrived to rush the unsuspecting victim to the hospital. Obviously, lawsuits were filed—but you may be surprised to hear who was finally sued. It was the telephone company. You read it correctly. The phone company was sued for not building a booth strong enough to withstand the onslaught of a drunk driver hitting it with his automobile!

Do you see what we are saying to people with this court decision? We are affirming that the "poor" driver (under the influence of alcohol) couldn't help himself; that he is not ultimately responsible for the consequences of his behavior—even though he chose as an adult to drink and drive that day. We are affirming the same principle when we legislate that a bartender is responsible for how many drinks a consumer devours in his bar. When do we begin taking responsibility for our own lives and begin doing what is right? When will we stop saying, "It wasn't my fault"?

Responsibility is what spiritual leadership is all about, but even then it isn't complete until we have passed it on to those under our care.

What are two ways you could take more responsibility for the health of your relationship with your partner/family? How about your friends/co-workers?

Let's Set a Goal!

Based on the biblical example we've just seen, we can identify a goal for ourselves as we become mentors in our relationships. The "GOAL" for a spiritual mentor should be:

G – *Godliness.* Your character and conduct, even when no one's watching.

O – *Objectivity.* You can see strengths and weaknesses clearly.

A – *Authenticity.* You are real, transparent, and open.

L – *Loyalty.* You are committed to your partner.

Beware of Potential Pitfalls

Very few men attempt this role of mentor without encountering some resistance. Every husband I worked with in our initial "pilot" group on spiritual leadership discovered this firsthand. Their wives weren't accustomed to Christlike mentoring and guidance, and now it was suddenly introduced to them. The change alone brought apprehension on their part. Later, I began to see the root issues. When there is resistance on the woman's part, it is generally a result of either the man's wrong motives and methods, or the woman's hesitation to be challenged or exhorted by a male.

Assuming your motives are pure and your methods are marked by humility, the woman's resistance and hesitation may be defined in Genesis 3:16. This Scripture describes the broken state of spiritual leadership (resulting from the fall of mankind) within the context of husbands and wives. Note the word "desire" in verse 16: "Your desire will be for your husband."

It is also used in Genesis 4:7 regarding the desire sin has for us. The word means "yearning for control." The woman will yearn for control, as a result of our present human state (3:16). Sin will also yearn to control mankind (4:7). In both uses of the word, God says that man must instead assume responsibility and lead. We cannot become passive.

Let me reiterate what is at issue. It is not that the man is sharper, more intelligent, or more talented. Often, the wife is indeed sharper than her husband in several areas. But being a mentor simply means that the male is *secure* enough to spot strengths and weaknesses, then allow her to flourish where she is sharper. He is to develop her in her "gift" areas, even if it simply means encouraging her and turning her loose to grow in them.

Unfortunately, this scenario seems to be the exception rather than the rule in many homes. We men are frequently insecure. What's more, because support/affirmation is absent, the woman develops a resistant heart to *any* mentoring from the man. Let me give you an analogy. Driving along a freeway one night, a woman noticed the headlights of a huge semi-truck tailgating her much too closely. She sped up, but so did the truck. She became afraid and drove even faster. Finally she exited the freeway and raced toward a nearby gas station. The truck followed her in. She leaped from her car and ran into the garage, where onlookers stood.

The truck driver then climbed down from his cab, walked to her car and pulled a would-be rapist from her back seat! The trucker had spotted the man from his higher vantage point and had determined to save the woman from harm. The woman, in essence, was running from the wrong man.

In a similar way, the protegé may run from or resist the help of a mentor, because of different vantage points and a misunderstanding of motives. And too often we give up our attempts to mentor our wives, because helping them is just too much of a hassle. According to my good friend Kent Askew, the problem in a nutshell is:

- Men want leadership without love.
- Women want security without submission.

It seems to me that we naturally run from this kind of much-needed accountability. It requires enormous amounts of commitment and honest communication. We are much too interested in maintaining a façade; we're more concerned with what we appear to be than what we really are. A few years ago, a private plane was flying across the Midwest. During the flight, the control tower noticed the plane was not sticking to its flight plan and attempted to make contact. They failed. Unknown to them, everyone onboard that plane was unconscious from lack of oxygen. No communication was possible. The plane ended up flying over the Atlantic Ocean and, when fuel ran out, finally went down. Everyone onboard died.

It's a tragedy. But the same kind of scenario occurs to people spiritually on a regular basis. We leave the flight plan, but the plane looks fine on the outside. No one could guess by watching that anything was wrong that day—and there was no communication. Ouch. That sounds awfully familiar.

THINK IT OVER/WRITE IT DOWN . . .

Give some thought to the status of your relationships, particularly the one with your partner. Think over how well you mentor in those relationships.

What are some strengths you can affirm in your partner?

What are some weaknesses you can help improve in your partner?

How might you mentor her (or your family) in both the strong areas and needy areas of growth?

What's the most conducive atmosphere for your partner to respond to your (or anyone's) attempts to develop her?

Some Final Practical Suggestions

1. Invest time and energy in this. Spend some time discussing this concept of mentoring with your partner. Have her share her perceptions of her strengths, weaknesses, and openness to this process.

2. Know yourself. If you're going to help others in their growth, you must know your own strengths, weaknesses, and personality traits. Good mentors always do.

3. Cultivate generosity. Good mentors have learned to be givers in relationships and realize that it is more blessed (and natural) to give than receive.

4. Study leadership. Read books and talk with people who can teach you how to be a better leader. You need to understand leadership issues. Good mentors always have mentors.

5. Initiate vulnerability. If you want an intimate, transparent, teachable partner and family, start practicing those qualities yourself. This accelerates the growth process.

6. Model character. If you want to pass on a trait or skill, remember: First you do it, then you do it as the protegé observes, then he does it as you observe, then he does it—whether you're there or not.

7. Pray for vision. Ask God to help you see His purposes for your partner, family, friends and co-workers to help you really believe in them. Ask Him to build in you the qualities of a good mentor:
   - Patience with people (Long-suffering)
   - Ability to see the big picture (Vision)
   - Commitment to relationships (Accountability)
   - Enjoyment in giving (Generosity)

- Strong personal discipline (Character)
- Good communication (Communicative)
- Understanding of others (Discernment)

As a mentor you must be committed to three things: a person, a process, and a purpose. Those in our families and spheres of influence will reflect whether we made this commitment. When Woodrow Wilson was president of Princeton University, he spoke these words to a parents' group:

> I get many letters from you parents about your children. You want to know why we people up here in Princeton can't make more out of them and do more for them. Let me tell you the reason we can't. It may shock you just a little, but I am not trying to be rude. The reason is that they are your sons, reared in your homes, blood of your blood, bone of your bone. They have absorbed the ideals of your homes. You have formed and fashioned them. They are your sons. In those malleable, moldable years of their lives you have forever left your imprint upon them.[2]

Developing a Lifestyle

- Memorize 1 Corinthians 13:4–7.

  > Love is patient, love is kind. It does not envy, it does not boast, it is not proud. It is not rude, it is not self-seeking, it is not easily angered, it keeps no record of wrongs. Love does not delight in evil but rejoices with the truth. It always protects, always trusts, always hopes, always perseveres.

- Discuss with your partner God's description of the male/female tension in Genesis 3:16. What are some ways you can address the female tendency to resist leadership, and the reason women often want to exercise authority? What are some ways you can address your tendency to "drop the ball" in your leadership role?

- Isolate one strength in your partner, and begin *this week* to affirm that strength in her.
- Isolate one weakness in your partner, and begin praying *daily* this week for God to begin developing this quality in her.
- Take responsibility this week for an area of your relationship that you have been avoiding.

8

The Spiritual Leader as a Manager

There are certain managerial functions we are called to perform as spiritual leaders.

United States history is full of intriguing stories. Many of them surround the men who have served as President of this great land of ours. One such story concerns a man you may not have heard of.

President-elect Zachary Taylor was scheduled according to the Constitution to take office on March 4, but he refused to be inaugurated because the day was a Sunday. Politicians pleaded in vain for the devoutly religious Taylor to change his mind.

The Constitution forbade current President James K. Polk from remaining another day. There was no alternative but for the Senate to elect a President to serve from Sunday noon to Monday noon, the time rescheduled for Taylor to take office. The senators chose David Rice Atchison, the head of the Senate.

However, the last week of the Polk administration was so hectic for Senator Atchison that he retired late Saturday evening after instructing his landlady not to awaken him for any reason.

She followed his orders. Senator Atchison slept through Sunday and on into Monday, past the time his twenty-four-hour term had ended. He slept through his entire term of office!

Unfortunately, this humorous account illustrates my first few years as a husband. I was sleeping through my office as a spiritual leader (figuratively speaking, of course). I was ignorant and often in a spiritual slumber when it came to domestic management in my home. I wish someone had shared with me what I'm about to share with you in this final chapter on being a "manager."

We must concede immediately that people don't want to be *managed*—they want to be *led*. Nonetheless, there are certain managerial functions we are called to perform as spiritual leaders. Again, we are models, ministers, mentors, *and* managers.

You've Joined the Priesthood!

This final chapter summarizes the essence of your task as a spiritual leader. As we discuss your role as a manager in your home, I believe the most vivid biblical analogy of what a spiritual leader should be for his family is the role of the priest. As managers, we must learn how to be priests in our homes. Let's examine this biblical picture for a moment. The office of a priest was a sacred one, and was coveted by Jewish men throughout both Old and New Testaments. It was a privileged and reverenced position, as well as a fearful and awesome one. Note some initial insights about the priesthood:

- Priests served in the temple regularly in the presence of God.
- They were responsible for making sacrifices on behalf of the people.
- They were considered spiritual role models for Jewish boys.

- They were a "type" of Christ—who now serves as our High Priest.

THINK IT OVER/WRITE IT DOWN . . .

Are you initially overwhelmed by this idea of being a priest to your family? Why or why not?

What do you think will be your greatest challenge in fulfilling this role, from your present understanding?

The Chief Functions of a Priest

The role of a priest can be distilled into two primary functions:

- To represent God to the people
- To represent the people (their needs) to God

As the spiritual leader to your partner and family, you have these same primary functions to fulfill. The Latin root for the term *priest* means "bridge-builder"—bringing the people and God together as a sort of bridge or middle-man between the two. Far too often, the connotations of the term *priesthood* have been just the opposite. It has served to alienate people from God by elevating the clergy role beyond the average person's reach. This is wrong. The priest is called to build bridges, not barricades. It's that simple.

In fact, the simplicity of this definition should encourage you. A married couple, Gary and Marsha, recently approached me, distraught over Gary's inability to perform as a spiritual leader in the home. They both agreed he was a failure. I told them to come back in a week, after they had each individually made a list of what they thought a spiritual leader was supposed to do.

When they returned a week later, each had formed a list that, frankly, didn't surprise me. Each had such a complex, lofty ideal of what a spiritual leader was to do that no one short of Superman could have lived up to it!

After discussing this simple biblical analogy of the priesthood, both breathed a sigh of relief. Marsha was relieved that Gary was really "normal" and that her unrealistic expectations were just that. Gary was relieved to think that he really *could* live up to the role of a biblical spiritual leader.

You are a priest. As a result of that position, your partner/family should benefit by seeing more clearly, loving more dearly, and following more nearly the personal and intimate God you know. Megan was in kindergarten when she finger-painted for the first time. Her teacher was observing each student's artwork when she paused to look at Megan's. The painting was completely abstract and it was difficult to tell just what it was supposed to be. So the teacher asked her what it was. Megan responded, "I'm painting a picture of God." The teacher smiled patronizingly, then explained, "Megan, no one knows what God looks like." To which Megan said with great resolve, "Well, they will when I'm done!"

It is my prayer that when you're "done" implementing the ideas in this chapter, people will better know what God looks like.

Does God Really Take This Stuff Seriously?

Before proceeding, let's look at the scriptural basis for this role we have. Does God really take seriously this business of our being a priest to our families? You bet He does. Let's confirm this by looking at two men in Scripture who *didn't* handle their roles so well: Eli and Lot.

TRUTH IN A NUTSHELL: 1 Samuel 2:12–36 (Eli)

Please get your Bible and read this passage carefully. You will meet a man who performed well on his job—but at the expense of his home.

Eli teaches us some simple but profound priority-principles. Jot them down as you answer the following questions.

THINK IT OVER/WRITE IT DOWN . . .

Eli was a priest at the altar in Shiloh as a vocation. He carried out that task satisfactorily. However, he failed to be a priest in his own home. What is the evidence of this?

Why do you suppose performing his job as a priest at Shiloh wasn't enough in God's eyes? What does this say about God?

What was God's response to Eli for his neglect to be a priest in his home?

Explain how Eli could have been such a fine priest in public but produce such a miserable home setting.

TRUTH IN A NUTSHELL: Genesis 13 and 19 (Lot)

As you read these two chapters dealing with a gentleman named Lot, note his failure at being a spiritual leader, a priest, to his own family. Again, he was a fine public servant to the community but a failure in his home.

Lot's Five Fatal Mistakes

1. **Emphasis.** He placed emphasis on financial rather than spiritual prosperity (Genesis 13:8–11).

2. **Environment.** He expected his family to live in Sodom and not be like the Sodomites (Genesis 13:12, 13).

3. **Expectation.** He thought he could change society without taking a stand (Genesis 19:1–11).

4. **Example.** He felt his family would accept his words instead of his lifestyle (Genesis 19:12–14).
5. **Entanglements.** He didn't realize how much the world had ensnared them all (Genesis 19:12–26).

Each of these mistakes are ones that Lot probably could have and would have corrected had he noticed them. But, while he would never admit it, he had slowly drifted into a spiritual anemia; he was numb to the voice of God. He didn't even see the imminence of death until the last minute. His predicament reminds me of how wolves were once killed by Eskimos in the northern parts of Canada. The Eskimos would coat a sharp knife with animal blood, and then freeze it. Once frozen, they would repeat the process again and again until several coats of blood were hardened on the blade. Then they would place the knife into the cold ground, with the blade sticking up in the air. At night, wolves would sniff it out and begin licking the frozen blood. Their desire grew as they continued past the outer layers. Finally, in their passion to get every drop, they continued to lick the bare blade, not realizing they were now cutting their own tongues and consuming their own blood. (Pardon the grotesque details of this analogy, would you?) As you may have guessed, the Eskimos would arrive in the morning to find the wolf dead from loss of blood.

What a vivid analogy of what Lot's own sin and blindness were capable of doing to him. Similarly, we can become consumed with our own agenda and fleshly desires, only to see God's purpose for our life slip through our fingers.

THINK IT OVER/WRITE IT DOWN . . .

Why do you think Lot got so caught up in "performing" for his community that he completely missed his responsibility at home?

What were some evidences that Lot didn't really care for the spiritual growth of his family?

Lot's conduct toward the other men of Sodom displayed his absolute anemic spiritual condition. Not only was he numb to the needs of his family, but he grew to be perverted like the other Sodomites. What could he have done to avoid this?

Imagine for a moment what might happen if just those people who've read this material decided they would become practicing priests to their families. What kind of influence might that have on other families? Churches? Communities? It really doesn't take much to make a difference. Revivalist John Wesley saw four out of every five taverns close down in England as a result of his "Methodist movement." Yet, historians tell us that only 1½ to 2 percent were actually involved in the movement. It doesn't take much. Umai was a man who led a revolution in Tinnevelly, India years ago. What makes his revolution so significant is that Umai was a deaf-mute who could speak only with sign language! His critics simply said, "Never underestimate the power of a fanatic." I say, "Never underestimate the power of a man with a purpose."

Four Necessities of Your Priesthood

As a fellow struggler who has devoted a good portion of my adult life to the study of spiritual leadership, I am convinced that there are four requirements in your life if you are going to be an effective priest to your partner and family. Indicate how you are doing in each area, on a scale of 1 (poor) to 10 (excellent).

1. **You must believe in and love yourself.**

   1 2 3 4 5 6 7 8 9 10

2. **You must believe in and love your family.**

   1 2 3 4 5 6 7 8 9 10

3. **You must believe in and love your role.**

   1 2 3 4 5 6 7 8 9 10

4. **You must believe in and love your Lord.**

   1 2 3 4 5 6 7 8 9 10

What improvements need to be made? What is your plan to make these improvements?

Let me take a moment to encourage you. God is calling you to a role that is absolutely feasible. It is a thrilling adventure, but it doesn't have to be complex or overwhelming. This role of priesthood is not supposed to be a source of anxiety, but of joy and fulfillment. Be human. Be real. Be natural. The most successful spiritual leaders I know handle things very naturally. They are warm. They are themselves. God never calls you to be anyone but yourself. With all of your failures, flops and fumbles, He calls you to simply use the abilities you have to fulfill this role. Maintain this balanced perspective.

Your family will respect this authentic approach more than a contrived piety. Learn to laugh at yourself. One of the greatest lessons I've learned as a leader is to not take myself too seriously. Did you catch that? There is a real difference between taking God and His work seriously, and taking yourself seriously. If we're honest, most of us are comical, haphazard creatures wanting desperately for our world to take us seriously. I think it would do us good to humble ourselves and assume the posture of a student before God the rest of our lives.

I made this decision long before I ever thought about spiritual leadership. I look back on my life and laugh at the hilarious predicaments I fell into, even as a pastor. One evening, while I was working on my theology degree in northern Oklahoma, I borrowed a friend's car to get to the church. My car was in the body shop, where it had been off and on most of that year. Returning home, I noticed the roads were icy and slick as a result of the snowy weather that day. It was late and I was tired as I hunted for a parking space on campus. The good news is, I did find a space; the bad news is, my front wheels got stuck on an ice patch as I entered it. I labored to remember what to do in such a situation. (Remember, I came from sunny San Diego.)

I finally recalled that I was taught to rock the car back and forth until it dislodged from the ice. So I got out and went to work. Again, the good news is, I did free the car from the ice patch. The bad news is, I failed to notice I was pushing the car on a slight incline—downhill! I panicked for a second as I helplessly watched that huge old Chevrolet Impala slowly roll away, down the incline. Quickly, I darted into action, chasing my runaway car.

More good news and bad news. The good news: I *did* catch the bumper of that car. The bad news: I was now skiing along that icy lot holding onto that bumper with all of my strength! To this day, I am certain that Impala had radar attachments and scoped out the most expensive foreign sports car in the area—because that's exactly what it hit at the bottom of the hill. All I could do was slump to the ground and reflect on the fact that not only was my car in the body shop, but soon so would my friend's Impala be, as well as that expensive, foreign sports car!

There. Now do you suddenly feel much better about yourself? I have concluded that often the best response I can make is to laugh at myself. After all—everyone else does.

A Practical Look at Your Priesthood

Before concluding this section on the priestly role of spiritual leadership, I'd like to give you a few practical suggestions on how you might fulfill the two functions of a priest. These are not comprehensive lists, but I hope they at least bring some ideas to mind. The key is not method, but principle. Which ideas you implement are not as important as the fact that you implement something.

Obviously, this list can be modified and used in your workplace, church or among close friends, whether you are married or single. I challenge you to become an active "priest" in the lives of others.

Function One: To Represent God To Your Family/Partner

1. Family Devotions

This involves sitting down with your family on a consistent basis to discuss items that are meaningful and important: to share the things that are on the minds of family members and, of course, to share Scripture with each other. Some Christian book stores carry materials full of ideas for these times. This experience can build tremendous memories for the future, and can be a source of security and strength. Family devotions should be:

- Planned and well-communicated
- A regular experience (you decide what is realistic)
- A discussion, with input from everyone

2. Prayer Times

This idea uses different life junctions, as well as daily events, to remind the family of the centrality of God's relationship to us. It simply involves pausing to pray and talk with God about a meaningful time in your lives, in the same way that crowds honor and remember our country by singing the national anthem before sporting events. You'll want to be creative so this experience doesn't become routine or trite. One family I know plays "Spin the Globe" each night. A child spins a globe and points to an area on it. When the globe stops its revolution, the family discusses and prays for whatever country the child is pointing toward. It's a fun little exercise. Here are a few times you could use for family prayer:

- At mealtimes
- Before trips
- Before or after events
- At bedtime

This relays the primacy of your dependence upon God, especially at key times in your life.

3. Expose Them to Godly Influences

It makes an impression on family members when you take them to a meaningful place, especially if it exposes them to significant people. Watch for interesting communicators, ministers, missionaries, or events that might build an enjoyable memory. A strategic time for children, incidentally, is around age twelve. This kind of experience with you could be a pivotal point in their lives.

- Take them to hear great speakers.
- Attend seminars and conferences with them.
- Take them to meet and pray with influential people.

4. Participate in Their Activities

Make your local church a family place, and participate together in events as you are able. Show enthusiastic support for specific programs they're a part of, even when there seems to be nothing particularly spiritual about it (such as a soccer game). Jesus designed the church to be people who build their lives and their families around purposeful togetherness as a body.

- Don't just drop them off—join them!
- Find church events you can participate in together.
- Support their activities with your attention.

5. Model Personal Disciplines Yourself

Remember, you can't lead anyone beyond where you have gone yourself. If they do happen to get beyond you, it's because they, or someone else, took initiative to make it happen. You are like a song being performed. Your lifestyle is the music; your words are the lyrics. Followers, especially children, become confused when the music and the lyrics don't coincide. Your faith needs to be expressed through every part of your life.

- Be visible.
- Be verbal.
- Be vulnerable.

During a church service, I saw a father carry his eleven-year-old son out of the auditorium. His son had been making disturbing noises, and was distracting the people near him by his fidgeting and squirming. I was moved emotionally when I saw him later in the foyer of the church, holding his son in his arms, stroking his hair. The boy has epilepsy, but the father showed no signs of embarrassment or humiliation by it all; he just kept whispering in his boy's ear, "I love you."

How I pray that kind of love would be passed on by husbands and dads today. But it cannot if it hasn't first been passed on to them. We're all in a cycle and tend to reproduce whatever has been given to us in our lives. You can't give it if you don't have it. We were interrupted during a worship service recently by loud weeping. It was coming from a twenty-eight-year-old man who had grown up in the church but had never really experienced what it's all about. That morning, as he wept, he was experiencing the Father-heart of God—the unconditional love of God—for the first time. Though he had received Christ by faith years before, it was during this worship experience that he and God really connected, and he has been different ever since. He had now had a "face-to-face" encounter with his Lord.

But that's not the end of the story. Not only is he a better person from encountering God like this, but he has the capacity to be a better husband and father in the days ahead. That is how the cycle is supposed to run.

Function Two: To Represent Your Family's/Partner's Needs To God

This function requires one simple but paramount activity on your part: *intercession.* You are called to build an effective intercessory prayer life on behalf of your family. Intercessory prayer is the highest form of prayer. It is bringing the needs of others to God for them; it is literally speaking to God on their behalf, representing them in His presence. This is best done when you do the following:

- Find a specific, daily time to pray.
- Locate a place of solitude.
- Use a prayer journal and list specific needs.

What To Pray For

- That God would raise them up to be great influences for Him.
- That God would guide them in future decisions, and give them wisdom.
- That God would protect them from the enemy.

- That God would open their spiritual eyes and keep their hearts soft.
- That God would give them a hungry heart and mind for Him.
- That God would lead them in discovering their role in His family.
- For children: That God would raise up and guide their future spouse.
- For spouse: That God would give insight and wisdom in the parenting process.

A boy living in New Jersey waits expectantly every year for the mailman to deliver a special letter to him on his birthday. His father, while dying of a terminal disease, knew the youngster would not have the benefit of his personal guidance and help as he grew into manhood. So he wrote his son a letter for each year, and left instructions for the letters to be sent so they would arrive annually on the proper date. A final envelope containing words of fatherly direction and advice will also be given to the son on his wedding day. Literally, the influence of the father is being felt long after he is gone.

This is also the power of intercessory prayer. Your prayers offered in faith on behalf of others long outlive your physical presence. Consequently, intercessory prayer is one of the wisest investments a spiritual leader will ever make.

9

A Final Thought

Well, you've done it—you have completed this material on becoming a spiritual leader!

I realize I have attempted to cover an enormous amount of territory in a short amount of space. I also understand we have just scratched the surface on the subject, and I am sure others will further address the issues in the future. In fact, I feel a little bit like the humorist who spoke these words:

> I fully realize that I have not succeeded in answering all of your questions . . .
>
> Indeed, I feel I have not answered any of them completely. The answers I have found only serve to raise a whole new set of questions, which only lead to more problems, some of which we weren't even aware were problems.
>
> To sum it all up . . . In some ways I feel we are confused as ever, but I believe we are confused on a higher level, and about more important things.

At any rate, let me take a moment and make some closing comments. I want to encourage you to make the content of these chapters a lifestyle. Here are a few tips on how to make the lessons a habit in your life:

- Continue seeing from time to time those people who have coached you in your spiritual leadership development, for accountability.
- Review the "Developing a Lifestyle" sections at the end of each chapter.

- Continue asking your partner what areas could be improved in your relationship.
- Continue to make your spiritual leadership development a daily item on your prayer list.

Remember, the journey hasn't ended with these chapters—it's only just begun!

To correspond with the author or to inquire about speaking engagements, readers may contact the author at the following address:

EQUIP
P.O. Box 7700
Atlanta, GA 30357
(888) 993-7847
x 3311

Notes

Chapter 2

1. Hybels, Bill. *Honest to God* (Grand Rapids, MI: Zondervan Publishing House, 1990), p. 40.
2. Laake, Deborah. "Wormboys: Is He a Wimp or Isn't He?" *The Reader* (November 4, 1983), p. 14.
3. Paraphrased from Zig Ziglar, *See You At the Top* (Pelican, 1984).

Chapter 3

1. Galli, Mark. "What Do Men Want?" *Leadership* (Winter 1991), p. 36.
2. Galli, "What Do Men Want?" p. 36.
3. "Dear Abby," *San Diego Union* (October 13, 1990).
4. Sanders, J. Oswald. *Spiritual Leadership* (Chicago, IL: Moody Press, 1980), pp. 184–89.
5. Swindoll, Charles. *Improving Your Serve* (Waco, TX: Word, Inc., 1981), pp. 52–53.
6. Sanders, J. Oswald. *Spiritual Leadership* (Chicago, IL: Moody Press, 1980), p. 19.
7. Hybels, Bill. *Honest to God* (Grand Rapids, MI: Zondervan Publishing House), pp. 51–52.

Chapter 4

1. Dawson, John. "The Father Heart of God," *Last Day Ministries Newsletter,* vol. 6, no. 1, pp. 14–18, 27–30.
2. Smalley, Gary and Trent, John. *The Blessing* (New York, NY: Pocket Books, 1986), p. 27.

Chapter 5

1. Indianapolis Tech *Challenge* newsletter (January 1983), p. 1.
2. Weinhouse, Beth. "How to Raise a Happy, Healthy Child: Kids and Stress," *Ladies Home Journal* (August 1988), p. 58.
3. Elliot, Elisabeth. *Passion and Purity* (Old Tappan, NJ: Fleming H. Revell Company, 1984), p. 97.

Chapter 6

1. Hodgin, Michael. *Parables, Etc.* (March 1991).
2. Balswick, Jack. *Why I Can't Say I Love You* (Waco, TX: Word, Inc., 1978), pp. 33–34.

Chapter 7

1. Campolo, Tony. *Who Switched the Price Tags?* (Dallas, TX: Word Publishing, 1986), p. 29.
2. Ton, Paul Lee. *Encyclopedia of 7,700 Illustrations* (Rockville, MD: Assurance Publishing, 1979), p. 960.